The Hour of Departure: Forces that Create Refugees and Migrants

HAL KANE

Jane A. Peterson, *Editor*

WORLDWATCH PAPER 125
June 1995

FINANCIAL SUPPORT is provided by The Nathan Cummings Foundation, the Energy Foundation, the Geraldine R. Dodge Foundation, The George Gund Foundation, W. Alton Jones Foundation, John D. and Catherine T. MacArthur Foundation, Andrew W. Mellon Foundation, Edward John Noble Foundation, Pew Charitable Trusts, Lynn R. and Karl E. Prickett Fund, Rockefeller Brothers Fund, Surdna Foundation, Turner Foundation, U.N. Population Fund, Wallace Genetic Foundation, and Frank Weeden Foundation.

PUBLICATIONS of the Institute include the annual *State of the World*, which is now published in 27 languages; *Vital Signs*, an annual compendium of the global trends—environmental, economic, and social—that are shaping our future; the *Environmental Alert* book series; *World Watch* magazine; and the *Worldwatch Papers*. For more information on Worldwatch publications, write: Worldwatch Institute, 1776 Massachusetts Ave., N.W., Washington, DC 20036; or fax 202-296-7365.

THE WORLDWATCH PAPERS provide in-depth, quantitative and qualitative analysis of the major issues affecting prospects for a sustainable society. The Papers are written by members of the Worldwatch Institute research staff and reviewed by experts in the field. Published in five languages, they have been used as a concise and authoritative reference by governments, nongovernmental organizations, and educational institutions worldwide. For a partial list of available Papers, see page 57.

DATA from all graphs and tables contained in this book, as well as from those in all other Worldwatch publications of the past year, are available on diskette for use with Macintosh or IBM-compatible computers. This includes data from the *State of the World* series, *Vital Signs* series, Worldwatch Papers, *World Watch* magazine, and the *Environmental Alert* series. The data are formatted for use with spreadsheet software compatible with Lotus 1-2-3, including Quattro Pro, Excel, SuperCalc, and many others. Both 3 1/2" and 5 1/4" diskettes are supplied. To order, send check or money order for $89, or credit card number and expiration date (Visa and MasterCard only), to Worldwatch Institute, 1776 Massachusetts Ave., NW, Washington, DC 20036. Tel 202-452-1999; Fax 202-296-7365; Internet: wwpub@igc.apc.org.

Table of Contents

Tables and Figures

Sections of this paper may be reproduced in magazines and newspapers with written permission from the Worldwatch Institute. For information, call the Director of Communication, at (202) 452-1999 or Fax: (202) 296-7365.

The views expressed are those of the author and do not necessarily represent those of the Worldwatch Institute, its directors, officers, or staff, or of its funding organizations.

89849

ACKNOWLEDGMENTS: I would like to thank Milton Leitenberg, Jocelyn Mason, Steven Hansch, Susana McCollom, and my colleagues at the Worldwatch Institute for their insights and for comments on the drafts of this paper. I would also like to thank Michael Renner for valuable project oversight, and Jim Perry and Denise Byers Thomma for help with production and outreach.

HAL KANE is a principal author of the annual *Vital Signs: The Trends That Are Shaping Our Future* (1992, 1993, 1994 and 1995), coauthor of *Full House: Reassessing the Earth's Population Carrying Capacity,* and coauthor of the *State of the World 1995,* as well as many other publications. Other topics he has researched include international trade, debt, fisheries, tobacco, and infant mortality. He is frequently a guest on radio shows worldwide, and has lectured at universities around the United States.

Introduction

Human migration, both voluntary and forced, ranks among the most volatile issues facing the world today. It is a barometer that registers our evolving, and sometimes declining, prospects for global security. The sooner we learn to read this gauge properly, the sooner we can come to terms with the changes that cast ever-increasing numbers of people adrift in the world.

Already about 125 million people live outside the countries where they were born—it is as if the entire population of Japan had packed up and left. Tens of millions more are on the move inside their borders, turning their backs on rural communities and heading into cities. Moreover, 4 million international refugees fled for their lives in 1994 alone, more than all the Spaniards who set out to colonize Latin America during their time of heaviest migration, the nineteenth and early twentieth centuries. In the future, these trends are likely to accelerate as the forces that push people from their homes grow more potent.[1]

Traditionally, relief agencies respond to the flow of refugees primarily with emergency rations and tents, while governments attempt to curb immigration with laws and border patrols. Although such short-term measures are crucial, they are often inadequate to meet current crises, much less future ones. But more importantly, whatever success they do have is likely to be only temporary, for they have no impact on the long-standing issues that precipitate many flows of refugees and migrants.

A common view holds that what precipitates migratory flows is persecution in the case of refugees, and job scarcity in the case of migrant labor. To be sure, these are common immediate catalysts that drive people out of their homes. But behind these particular factors lies the cumulative interplay of several rapidly intensifying pressures, population growth prominent among them. Land scarcity, for example, played a critical role in the recent eruption of war in Rwanda. And water scarcities have pushed millions of rural Chinese out over their thresholds. In virtually every instance of conflict or poverty today, factors like unmanageable population growth, unsustainable development, even disease and illiteracy have fermented over time in a volatile cocktail of insecurity. It is this combination of factors that ultimately brings people to the sometimes hopeful, but often desperate, hour of departure.[2]

Nevertheless, most governments do not even collect data relating to many of the trends that bring about departures. Indeed, they scarcely recognize environmental decline or demographic change as significant contributors to the conflicts and poverty people seek to escape. Even when useful data does exist—on population growth, or desertification, for example—people often do not make a connection between these pressures and the traumatic developments that finally tip the balance into migration. In effect, the symptoms—migration and flight—have blinded people to the root causes of crises. But to make people more secure in their homes (so that they can remain in them if they wish to) requires a deeper look at what is causing so many to move.

Steps that address the sources of insecurity pushing people into the outside world, especially when taken early, are by far the most cost-effective, not to mention the most humanitarian, way to approach the issue of involuntary migration. Investments in agricultural education or in community development loans that stave off food and employment shortages in rural areas act as an *economic insurance policy.* Such investments reduce the sums that relief organizations would have to expend later to help those who flee famine, and ease the future task of coping with pressures created by people who move to overcrowded cities. Early investments in stable communities also ward off the outflows of refugees that can threaten national security and the integrity of borders in neighboring nations, as well as the outflows of economic migrants that can trigger xenophobia in those countries.

The current pattern of waiting until emergencies unfold and then trying to help the victims is actually a source of despair, as the need for assistance always seems to overwhelm the supply of help. Ascribing wars like those of Rwanda or Somalia to "ancient ethnic animosities," also curtails hope by putting those conflicts outside the scope of the international community's ability to address them. Such problems are of course real, but it would be regrettable to focus on unsolvable problems at the expense of those that can be, if not solved, then at least mitigated. If, instead, we see the role that root causes play in migration, then we have a catalog of pressures that we can work to reduce.

The symptoms—migration and flight—have blinded people to the root causes of crises.

Fortunately, in many countries, from Bangladesh and India to Eritrea and Bolivia, a new view of migration is emerging, one that acknowledges the role of long-term pressures and espouses early action to encourage stability and security. Their policies exemplify effective steps, steps that can be taken only after a careful reading of the migration barometer.

From the Gulf States to Germany and the Americas and Australia, many countries have long depended on the talent and energy of immigrants to build their societies, and few would wish to interfere with voluntary migrants, the people who freely choose to move and are accepted abroad. But the many millions who move against their wishes, who would prefer to improve their lot without leaving their homes or breaking up their families, ought to be enabled to remain where they are—not only for their own sake, but also for the sake of their home communities, some of which have lost so much muscle and brain power that they are seriously hampered in their efforts to move forward. At the same time, receiving countries also need some protection from the even more massive influx likely to come if the world continues on its present course of mounting financial inequities, declining environmental health, and rapid population growth.

Imagine a hundred million souls—more than the total population of most countries—floating from countryside to city and from one town to another, as they are now *inside* China. That movement, and the economic change and population growth that led to it, have resulted in roads being built so fast and in so many new directions that the mapmakers cannot keep up with them.[3]

A similar inability to keep up with change also applies to the way we think of migration and the factors that set hundreds of millions of people in motion. So many people are on the move today, driven by so many different pressures, that our old assumptions about population movement may be as out of date as the Chinese guidebooks that show rice fields where today small cities stand.

The Shared Roots of Departure

To understand what makes people leave home, it is important to look not only at the different classifications of departees, but also at the commonalities—the shared roots of departure. Whether they be considered "official" refugees, internally displaced peoples, oustees, illegal or legal migrants, many people were actually torn away from their homes by intersecting problems: land scarcities, out-of-control population growth, ethnic disputes, and political manipulation, among others. (See Table 1.) The immediate cause of departure may have been war or poverty, but war and poverty themselves invariably grow out of years of mounting pressures that finally combine in a mixture that propels people over the edge.

In a sense, migrants and refugees are the same people, subjected to varying intensities and manifestations of the same problems. Migrants walk away more or less voluntarily while refugees have little choice but to run. But the same job and resource scarcities that directly push migrants out, for example, also indirectly eject refugees when they contribute to the anger or fears behind the persecution from which refugees flee. And, had they opted to stay, some people who migrated in the past would have become refugees today—assuming that their countries continued down a path of worsening problems.

TABLE 1

People on the Move, 1995

Category	Number	Type
	(millions)	(for the most part)
Cumulative		
Official Refugees	23	External, forced
Internal Refugees	27	Internal, forced
Illegal Migrants	>10	External, voluntary
Legal Migrants	100	External, voluntary
Per Year		
Oustees	10 every year	Internal, forced
Rural-to-Urban Migrants	20 to 30 every year	Internal, voluntary

Total: Approx. 35 million people moving within their countries every year.

Total: Approx. 125 million people outside their countries of origin.

Source: Worldwatch based on sources in endnotes 1, 37, and 42.

Table Note: With the exception of the Official Refugee figure, all these figures are broad approximations. *Official refugees* are those registered by the United Nations as having fled persecution and those under the protection of the U.N. High Commission for Refugees (UNHCR). *Internal refugees* are people who are in similar conditions but who have not crossed international borders and so cannot be official refugees. *Illegal migrants* often move for economic reasons, but not always; no reliable counts exist for their numbers, hence the figure here is a gross estimate. *Legal migrants* mostly move to find jobs and earn incomes abroad, but not always. *Oustees* are people moved by public works projects, usually remaining inside their countries. *Rural-to-Urban migrants* move to cities within their own countries, especially to find better livelihoods; no comprehensive data exist to chronicle their moves. These types are explained in more detail in the course of the paper.

Likewise, internal and international migration have much in common; in fact, internal migration is sometimes a first step to emigration. All these movements of people derive from the failure of societies to meet the fundamental needs and aspirations of their citizens, for safe places to live, or for jobs, for example. Understanding those pressures provides insights into the situations of refugees and migrants alike and puts us in a position to respond to them.

Occasionally the immediate reason people move is straight-forward, as when hundreds of thousands of people escaped the "Zone of Estrangement" around Chernobyl, Ukraine, after its nuclear plant spewed radiation. But, contrary to the impression created by accounts in the popular press, single causes are rare.[4]

It is significant that countries with stable populations and high levels of education and public health demonstrate a resilience against war and overt persecution and rarely experience refugee and migrant outflows. Many countries ravaged by high infant mortality, low literacy, eroding farmland, and hunger, on the other hand, are highly susceptible to the despots, the politically motivated bigotry, and the extremist politics that eventually force people out, and in fact they have recently seen people leave at record rates.

The migration situation is analogous to the spread of a dis-ease, where the causes of infection are often complex and obscure. Malnourished people, for instance, suffer from weak-ened immune systems and eventually lose their ability to fight infection. They rarely die of starvation, but malnourishment nevertheless underlies the illnesses that kill them. Likewise, lack of proper sanitation increases the likelihood of a cholera epi-demic or the spread of other diseases. In such instances, disease is only the final element in a series of deeper difficulties.

Much of Africa's migration today illustrates similar connec-tions between stresses. The continent has no more per capita income today than it did at the end of the seventies, and at 92/1,000 its infant mortality rate is the highest in the world. Despite the fact that grain yields have more than doubled, Africa's grain production per person is lower today than it was in 1950 because of its high crude birth rate (5.9 children per woman). At 118 kilograms per person, annual grain production is only around half as much as would be required, without imports, to keep people healthy.[5]

Famine is sufficient to drive millions to relief camps and across borders. Often, however, famine combines with political extremism and armed conflict to force even more people to move. The fighting worsens famines because people cannot stay on their farms and because soldiers steal food; and the social disintegration that follows acute hunger and dislocation of people fuels violence because people's resistance against demagoguery weakens when their social networks are dispersed. (See Table 2.)

Thus, famine and conflict are tied together, and their combination produces far larger migrations than either would alone. Somalia, for instance, is a place where these problems have intersected, with disastrous consequences. Since early 1994, most fighting has occurred outside Mogadishu in the farm belt. And yet, according to some Somalia analysts, the U.S. and the U.N. paid little attention to one of the underlying causes of conflict, the struggle to control the nation's best farmland, which is coveted by the warlords. Actually, Somalia's conflict is the continuation of a 100-year-old movement of major Somali clans southward from nomadic grazing areas that have been becoming more and more overpopulated. Today, resident minority tribes such as the Gosha have been dispossessed of their land. Half a million Somalis were refugees in neighboring countries in 1993, and some 700,000 were internally displaced. Behind their wanderings lay not just fighting among clans but also long-term population growth and land scarcity.[6]

Famine and conflict are tied together, and their combination produces far larger migrations than either would alone.

In Vietnam, overcrowding has caused whole communities to move. Few places are poorer than neighboring Cambodia, yet that country's open spaces and fish-filled rivers have proved irresistible to hundreds of thousands of inhabitants of overcrowded Vietnamese villages over the years (although now many are fleeing an "ethnic cleansing" campaign by the Khmer Rouge guerrillas).[7]

Poverty and environmental degradation often create scarcities that push people out of the regions where they live. Exhausted supplies of firewood and timber for heating and

TABLE 2

Categories of the Uprooted

Immediate Cause of Departure	Observation/Description
Persecution	Causes people to leave countries when they are able. Qualifies people for official refugee status and aid abroad if the persecution was based on race, religion, nationality, or political opinion.
Warfare	Causes both international and internal displacement by force. Many of these people qualify as official refugees abroad. Within their own countries, though, assistance may not be able to reach them.
Lack of Jobs	Causes both international and internal migration, but these individuals do not qualify as refugees because the cause of their moving was economic. Includes both legal and illegal migrants who moved voluntarily.
Environmental Degradation	Sometimes directly causes departure, but usually joins with other stresses in a cocktail of problems that force people out. They do not qualify as refugees, and often do not cross national borders.
Redrawing of Borders	Causes many people to move out of newly created countries and into others where they feel more secure or more at home. Creates migrants out of people who formerly were at home. They become voluntary migrants who leave for political or economic reasons. They do not qualify for assistance unless they were persecuted.
Forced Settlement	Moves people against their will, usually to make way for infrastructure like roads and power plants, but also sometimes to change the ethnic or political balance of a region, or for other reasons. These people usually remain within their home country and sometimes receive compensation from the governments or organizations that moved them.

TABLE 2, CONTINUED

Categories of the Uprooted

Immediate Cause of Departure	Observation/Description
Famine	Forces people to look for food in other regions. Caused by the interplay of several factors, especially land scarcities and environmental degradation, wars that prevent farmers from producing, inequities of ownership, and inefficiencies of production. People who flee famine sometimes receive humanitarian assistance, but not refugee assistance unless they prove that they were persecuted.
Poverty	Requires people to look elsewhere for livelihoods and the means to take care of their families. Even many people who have jobs lack the buying power and resources to survive or prosper. They become economic migrants when they look for adequate opportunities elsewhere.
Political Disem- powerment	Forces people to leave if they cannot protect them-selves or provide for their families. People unable to vote or participate in public life or business have little ability to take care of their needs. Unless they can demonstrate in court that they or a group they belong to was singled out for persecution, they receive no assistance when they leave.

Source: Worldwatch.

cooking and building, depleted wells, overcrowding in houses and schools, and a lack of electricity all plague poor regions. These scarcities often band together to form a cycle of inadequacy. Felled trees, for example, no longer anchor soil, which washes away and clogs rivers, and the disrupted flows of water cause further soil erosion and disrupt harvests of fish. In rural areas where people directly depend on the soil and water and forests for sustenance, poverty is essentially an environmental trend. These people are usually cash poor, yet so long as they are natural-resource rich, they can remain home and prosper. But when people flee poverty they are often fleeing environmental impoverishment—after the topsoil blew away or the well ran dry—in places without a rural economy that can offer them alternative sources of livelihood.

Any human migration on a monumental scale may begin with something like the partition of a corn field. From there, tensions grow as plots of land become too small to feed families, and as young workers leave those inadequate fields to look for scarce jobs elsewhere. These tensions culminate with exploitative politics by people who play on insecurity to build hatred and factionalism for their personal gain. This has been the story of many who fled famine, including hundreds of thousands in Haiti, Somalia, Burundi, and, most recently, Rwanda.

In Rwanda, the most densely populated country in Africa, the partition of farmland is behind some of the hatred that erupted in 1993 into some of the deadliest violence of modern times. The country steadily expanded the amount of land in crop production until the mid-eighties, at which point virtually all arable land was in use. Today, the average farm size is less than half a hectare, and as land is subdivided among male heirs, plot size is dwindling. The practice of fallowing has virtually disappeared, manure is in short supply because many farms are too small to provide fodder for cattle, and yields have been declining. These are threatening trends to people with too little land to feed their children, just the sort that arouse fear, jealousy, and hatred.[8]

The implosion of Rwanda illustrates these issues. In the wake of the violence, some 2.1 million Rwandans remained refugees at the end of 1994. But the speed with which the crisis broke was misleading. To be sure, the refugees fled hatred between two groups of people, as the mass media reported. But that hatred grew in part out of Rwanda's colonial history and deep, long-standing tensions.[9]

Not only past war, but even epidemic illnesses and other pressures contributed to the Rwandan conflict. Like its neighbor Uganda, Rwanda was one of the countries hit first and hardest by AIDS. And years of internal warfare had already taken many casualties before the current tragedy. The generation of people 20 to 40 years old bore a disproportionate number of the deaths from both causes, so that large numbers of boys and young men lost their parents, which left them with dim prospects for fulfilling lives. They were more readily recruited as soldiers as a result. Tina Malone, who organizes the relief effort for Catholic Relief Services, calls these children "cannon fodder—the stuff from which you can make a militia."[10]

The tensions created by widespread orphaning were compounded by class friction between Hutus and Tutsis. During colonial times, Tutsis were the favored group, with the result that they became better educated and richer than the Hutus. As happened in the French Revolution, class resentment became a motive for slaughter. And indeed, a significant part of the fighting and killing that took place in Rwanda involved poorer members of either group attacking richer members of the same group in social, political, and class struggle.

Hatred grew in part out of Rwanda's colonial history and deep, long-standing tensions.

Tutsi is not exactly the name of an ethnic group: historically it meant "people who own cattle." And Hutu meant "people who farm." Despite class differences, however, intermarriage between the groups is widespread, and has been for years. They speak the same language and share the same religion (Christianity). Although the potential for fighting was there, its outbreak was not inevitable—contrary to the impression given by press reports. Propaganda spread by disenfranchised factions lit the fuse.[11]

Malone explicitly connects some of these issues in her analysis of the Rwandan disaster. "People can easily turn around and blame misfortune on the fact that there's not enough land to go around," she says. "And then someone puts the idea into their heads about Hutus and Tutsis, and it starts." Had it not been for the land scarcity and demographic disruption and related pressures, Rwandan society would have been more resilient.[12]

Lebanon offers an example of a place where rigid politics converged with demographic change to force people out. When the French established the state of Lebanon, they did so according to a rigid political structure based on demographic balance. At the time, half the population was Christian, mostly Maronite, and the other half was Muslim, with Sunni Muslims outnumbering Shiites. An unwritten but widely accepted "national pact" required that the Lebanese president be a Maronite, the prime minister a Sunni Muslim, and the speaker of parliament a Shiite. Parliament was to have a six-to-five ratio of Christians to Muslims.[13]

By the seventies, Christians comprised only a little more than one-third of the population, while Muslims and Druse (a smaller Islamic sect) accounted for the remaining two-thirds. The Shiites were the largest community and the poorest group in the society. When the new majority demanded a greater share of the power, the Maronites resisted, and they formed private armies to ensure the status quo. The Muslims and Druse established their own militias in response, and war eventually erupted. Although it was the militias that people fled from, behind the violence lay a rigid political system unable to accommodate a changing demographic balance and new demands to share power. More than a third of all Lebanese now live outside of Lebanon, largely as a result of this conflict.[14]

Overly rigid political systems often play a role in translating pressures into strife. As South Africa's new government has so far demonstrated, open political systems can head off some conflicts by adapting and making people feel represented. But in closed political systems, some groups feel disadvantaged and seek other outlets for their voices and needs.

Political abuses also contribute to political turmoil. At least in part, this is the case in Kenya, which has the least cropland per person of any country in Africa and the second least of any country in the world. Nomadic Masai tribespeople have attacked Kikuyu farmers, chasing them off their land and converting it to pasture. Yet many people believe that in Kenya, as in many countries, the source of conflict is a leader who needs to manipulate ethnic tensions in order to retain power—political manipulations pushed these tensions over the threshold into violence.[15]

Historically, civil wars have been closely tied to population growth and the accompanying pressures of environmental scarcity and social disruption. During the sixteenth and seventeenth centuries in Europe, for example, the dozen states with the fastest population growth rates all had revolts, while the states with slow population growth enjoyed peace, according to research by Jack Goldstone, a historian at the University of California at Davis. During the eighteenth and nineteenth centuries, the relationship continued.[16]

Using analysis of worldwide population trends, Goldstone explains the English Revolution of 1640 and the French Revolution of 1789, as well as a wave of revolts from 1600 to 1660 that stretched across Europe from the Netherlands through central Europe and Russia, to Ottoman Turkey and Ming China. According to Goldstone's theory, "Large agrarian states of this period were not equipped to deal with the impact of the steady growth of population that then

More than a third of all Lebanese now live outside of Lebanon.

began throughout northern Eurasia, eventually amounting to population increases in excess of the productivity gains of the land." Pressure on resources led to persistent price inflation, undermined the tax bases of many states, and caused financial crisis. Population growth also gave rise to rivalry and factionalism among elites by increasing the number of aspirants for coveted positions, and their demands were difficult to satisfy given the fiscal strains on the state.[17]

Although the patterns of economic and social disruption described by Goldstone appeared centuries ago, they could apply to parts of the world today, including West Africa. Then as now, long-standing and mounting tensions stemming from deeper sources such as population growth, rigid political systems, and resource scarcities underlay the particular pressures, like armed conflict, that ultimately made people leave home.

Particular Pressures: War and Persecution

As important as it is to explore root causes of population movement, an understanding of particular or immediate causes is still essential. Of these catalysts, war and persecution are two of the most fearsome, the proverbial last straws that turn many people into refugees. And like other factors that precipitate migration, they have become more complex and difficult to delineate in recent years.

As of December 31, 1994, some 23 million people qualified for international assistance as official refugees, an all-time record. (See Figure 1.) In 1989, the figure was 15 million. And as recently as the mid-seventies, only about 2.5 million people could claim refugee status—about the same number as in the fifties and sixties. These are the individuals who met the strict standard established in 1950 and 1951, and affirmed in 1967, by the United Nations, which defined refugees solely in terms of persecution: any person who "owing to well-founded fear of being persecuted for reasons of race, religion, nationality, membership of a particular social group, or political opinion, is outside the country of his nationality and is unable to...return to it." That narrow definition is a remnant of the Cold War. Its purpose was largely to weaken the former Soviet Union and other states within its domain by granting refuge to people who fled from them.[18]

These requirements for gaining refugee status receive considerable attention as officials and observers try to sort out which individuals deserve assistance and which do not. In fact, the U.N. definition only covers some of the people who need assistance. But for those who do qualify, the majority have one thing in common: their countries suffered from civil war.[19]

In 1995, of the 20 largest source countries of refugees in the world, 19 are embroiled in internal armed conflict. Thus it is clear that, while persecution is the officially accepted qualification for refugee status, in fact widespread internal warfare is the dominant contributor.[20]

Since 1945 there have been over 130 wars. Counting only those killed directly in the fighting, over 23 million people have perished. Including some of those who died as a result of war-related famine or illness, some 40 million have perished. By one

FIGURE 1

World Official Refugees, 1960–94

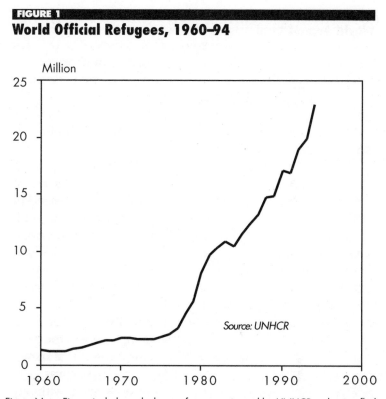

Figure Note: Figure includes only those refugees registered by UNHCR as having fled persecution.

analysis, the number of war deaths during this post-1945 period has been more than twice that in the 19th century and seven times that in the 18th century. With such deadly wars, the world's refugees have had good reason to flee.[21]

After the mid-twentieth century, warfare spread. From an average of 11 wars claiming over 1,000 lives at any one time during the fifties, the number of conflicts grew in the sixties to about 15, and then climbed in the late seventies and early eighties to over 30. (See Figure 2.) Part of the increase in the world's refugee population came during the years of the rise in warfare, in the late seventies and early eighties.[22]

Civilian losses accounted for half of all war-related deaths in the 1950s, but by the 1980s they added up to three-quarters, and

FIGURE 2

World Armed Conflicts, 1945–94

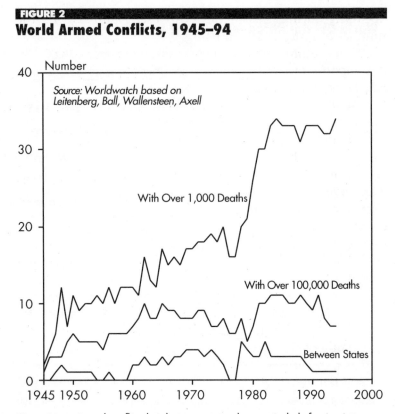

Figure Note: Armed conflict data between states does not include foreign interventions in civil wars, nor wars of independence from colonial rule.

in 1990, some 90 percent of war deaths were civilian, whereas in many past wars most casualties were soldiers. Indeed, UNICEF says that over the last 10 years, more children—some two million have died in civil strife. This trend is worsened by the fact that in some wars, such as Liberia's, many of the soldiers *are* children—in their early teens or younger.[23]

In part, this rising deadliness and increased targeting of civilians explains why the number of refugees continued to rise even after the number of wars stopped growing in the early nineties. The number of the most devastating conflicts—those that have taken over 100,000 lives—is actually declining during the nineties. (Also see Figure 2.) Yet the number of refugees is still rising.[24]

With hostilities playing such a major role in causing flight, it is important to understand the nature of today's wars, few of which take place between states. Rather, almost all are civil wars. Even the rare examples of conflicts that cross state borders are more cases of internal conflicts spilling over a border than instances of aggression between two countries. The war over Nagorno-Karabakh in Azerbaijan, for example, involves two countries, but it is essentially an internal secessionist struggle. And the Israeli occupation of south Lebanon is an extension of Israel's and Lebanon's internal conflicts.[25]

> **Over the last 10 years, more children—some 2 million—than soldiers have died in civil strife.**

The most recent war that clearly could be categorized as international was the Gulf war that followed Iraq's 1990-91 invasion of Kuwait. It provides evidence that wars to take foreign territory or to protect against external enemy aggression still do occur, though rarely.[26]

The failure of societies to hold themselves together, not external aggression, is the leading cause of flight today. By the count of the United Nations, of the 82 armed conflicts in the world between 1989 and 1992, only 3 flared up between countries. The rest occurred internally, often against a background of poverty, inequalities, and weak or rigid political systems. If these underlying stresses continue, and if this trend of internal war continues, it will almost certainly send refugees fleeing from problems that were held in check in the past, some of them prevented by Cold War geopolitics.[27]

Because today's wars rage inside countries, many people are exposed to harm who, in an international conflict, might be safe behind battle lines. Children and women, for example, are particularly vulnerable to internal war—and they make up a disproportionate part of refugee flows. Although roughly 80 percent of refugees worldwide are children and women, only about 70 percent of the population of the typical countries that send out refugees belong to those vulnerable groups.[28]

Political conflict has led some people to leave for rather eso-teric reasons. For instance, migrants can be created to be used as a tool of war. "Sending immigrants is the most effective way to colonize countries because it is less offensive than to send mil-itary expeditions and much less expensive," wrote Machiavelli, the sixteenth-century Italian philosopher. Perhaps the Chinese read his work. In any event, they have used double rations and doubled salaries to lure their citizens out of their homes, a form of "population transfer" designed as part of a strategy for quashing Tibetan nationalism. Chinese officials describe Tibet as a barren, inhospitable land. Nevertheless, areas that were populated entirely by Tibetans before 1950 are now predomi-nantly Chinese. At 7.6 million, the Chinese now outnumber the 6.1 million Tibetans still residing in their own homeland.[29]

Following an even more drastic policy, Saddam Hussein has used expulsion as a strategy for war against minorities in Iraq who might not support him. His military forced a million and a half Kurds into neighboring Turkey in 1991 during a three-week peri-od. For the same reasons, he also forced Shiite Muslims from southern Iraq into Iran. In this instance, it is nearly impossible to distinguish between war and persecution.[30]

Wars and flows of refugees are concentrated in certain parts of the world. Until 1993, Asia had the most refugees. But increasing warfare in Africa earned it that dubious honor in 1994. That same year, Europe also passed Asia to become the sec-ond largest refugee continent—mostly because of the war in the former Yugoslavia and the disintegration of the Soviet Union. Thus, for the first time since World War II, Europe is both receiv-ing and sending large numbers of refugees.[31] (See Figure 3.)

Overall, however, the concentration of hostilities and refugees in this half century has been in the Third World. In both the number of conflicts and the number of casualties, developing countries bear the heaviest burdens—well over 90 percent of each. Afghanistan stands at the head of the pack, having lost at the 1992 peak of flight 6.3 million individuals to migration. Of those, some 2.6 million had returned home by the end of 1994. Nevertheless, Afghanistan is still the world's largest source

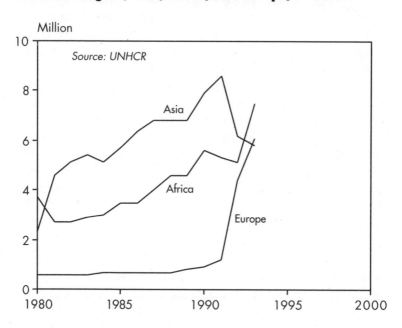

FIGURE 3

Official Refugees, Asia, Africa, and Europe, 1980–93

of war refugees. (See Table 3.) In percentage terms, however, it is the war in Liberia that has sent out the most escapees—nearly half of its 2.6 million people are now thought to live in exile (though most do not qualify as official refugees).[32]

Among the continents, Africa has the most armed conflict, but several of its wars have recently come to an end. A war in Mozambique that dates back to 1976 and may have taken a million lives has ended with a ceasefire that has held since 1993. After 30 years of fighting, Ethiopia is at peace, at least for the time being, and Eritrea today is a new country enjoying considerable national unity and optimism. It has taken steps toward achieving land redistribution and gender equality that could strengthen long-term peace. Angola and Chad, where civil war began in 1980 and 1965, respectively, both have encouraging prospects for peace. And, of course, the apartheid of South Africa has ended, after taking more than 18,000 lives during the 1990s alone.[33]

TABLE 3

Refugees Registered by UNHCR: Top Ten Countries of Origin, Circa Early 1995

Country of Origin	Main Countries of Asylum	No. of Refugees
Afghanistan	India/Iran/Pakistan/Russia	2,950,000
Rwanda	Burundi/Tanzania/Uganda/Zaire	2,125,000
Liberia	Cote d'Ivoire/Ghana/Guinea/ Sierra Leone	848,000
Somalia	Djibouti/Ethiopia/Kenya/Yemen	516,800
Eritrea	Sudan	425,400
Sudan	Ethiopia/Kenya/Uganda/Zaire	391,200
Azerbaijan	Armenia	334,900
Angola	Congo/Zaire/Zambia	325,500
Sierra Leone	Guinea/Liberia	311,100
Burundi	Rwanda/Zaire/Tanzania	271,000

Source: UNHCR, private communication, February 3, 1995.

The powerful pull of home is demonstrated by the large numbers of refugees who repatriated following the end of those wars in Africa (though some people repatriate only for lack of better opportunities). Some 1.2 million people have returned to Mozambique since the conflict's peak in 1992, all but 300,000 of those outside that country at that time. And out of one million at the peak of flight in 1989, about 600,000 have gone back to Ethiopia since 1991. About half a million refugees from Rwanda have returned home, though fears of continued fighting keep most refugees still abroad. Roughly half a million have repatriated to Burundi, and 400,000 to Somalia. These repatriations are large by historical standards. Not only are more people becoming refugees than in the past, but more are going home as well, making for a dynamic flow of people.[34]

Many analysts have hypothesized that warfare would spread in the world after the ending of the Cold War because Soviet and American influence had held other, long-simmering conflicts in check; others theorized that warfare would decline as the superpowers stopped supporting foreign proxy conficts. Indeed, several new wars did arise at the end of the Cold War, in particular in the former Yugoslavia and in Soviet Central Asia. And some others came to an end as military assistance was withdrawn by the superpowers, in Mozambique, Angola, Nicaragua, and El Salvador, for example. But the fact that the main increase in the number of wars raging in the world came earlier, during the late seventies and early eighties, suggests that the end of the Cold War is probably not the primary factor influencing the outbreak of warfare today.[35] (See Figure 2.)

One possible alternative explanation for the rise in hostilities during past years is the cumulative effect of decades of unsustainable development, the consequences and pressures of which have begun to undermine the well-being and security of many countries. In some of the poorer countries, such costs are felt widely and directly, and pressures begin to boil over. If unsustainable development is indeed a major cause of war, then the passing of Cold War politics will not have as large an effect as expected.

The end of the Cold War is probably not the primary factor influencing the outbreak of warfare today.

Worldwide, the number of wars rose slightly during 1994, reaching 34. And while several of those wars have now been resolved, possibly leading to more repatriation and less migration, the increasing *deadliness* of wars, especially to civilians, raises the possibility that hostilities will continue to drive larger numbers of refugees out of homes and across borders in the future.[36]

Failing the Official Refugee Test

The official insistence that only persecution—and, indirectly, warfare—enables people to qualify as refugees excludes many other crucial reasons why people today decide to leave home. Those who escape famine are denied refugee status, even though they had no choice but to leave or perish. Those who fear that they are losing the means to take care of their children do not qualify either, even though that prospect may be as terrifying as the threat of violence. Those who are expelled by natural disasters are also rejected. Yet all these people can find themselves with the same needs as official refugees.

Most of the people driven from home by forces other than war and persecution cannot enter other countries—and do not wish to. So they join the "internally displaced," those who flee involuntarily but remain in their home countries. Not counting people who move for economic reasons, the number of internally displaced is at least 27 million worldwide.[37]

The uprooted citizens who stay within their countries are often worse off than their counterparts abroad. Even when international aid agencies wish to help people adrift inside their own borders, these agencies do not usually have access inside national boundaries, so these victims go without help. Recently, the United Nations High Commission for Refugees (UNHCR) has become increasingly willing to help internal refugees, notably in the former Yugoslavia, but also in Mozambique, Azerbaijan, Tajikistan, and other places. (See Table 4.) Still, these operations must tiptoe around issues of sovereign control.[38]

Some other people who fail to qualify as official refugees do manage to cross a border into another country, but they do so illegally. The total number of illegal immigrants (most of whom moved to seek better economic opportunities, but some of whom fled out of fear) is unknown, but it probably amounts to at least 10 million.[39]

Land degradation and the threat of famine have ousted millions of people. In the Sahel drought between 1968 and 1973, for example, about 20 percent of Mauritania's population, more than 250,000 people, fled to towns when they could not feed themselves at home in rural areas. In the mid-eighties, another famine in the Sahel drove more than two million people out of Chad, Mali, Mauritania, Burkina Faso, and Niger. During those years, additional people left their homes in other countries in Africa, South and Southeast Asia, and around the world once they reached a point where they

TABLE 4

Internally Displaced Persons Registered by UNHCR, Circa Early 1995

Country	Number
Bosnia & Herzegovina	2,740,000
Mozambique	791,100
Azerbaijan	778,000
Croatia	520,000
Tajikistan	520,000
Afghanistan	290,000
Cyprus	265,000
Georgia	260,000
Angola	200,000
Armenia	150,000
Total	6,514,100

Source: UNHCR, private communication, February 3, 1995.

Table Note: The total number of the internally displaced is much larger. These are only the people recognized by the United Nations.

could no longer support themselves on their degraded farmland or outlast temporary droughts. By 1994, one-sixth of the population of Mali and Burkina Faso had been uprooted as a result of desertification.[40]

Most of these people are not classified as "internally displaced" or as illegal migrants because they did not flee political pressures or cross international borders. They lack classification altogether. Those who moved to cities could be put in the column of "rural-to-urban" migrants. Others just slip through the world's international data-gathering net.

Yet the numbers of these migrants are likely to increase as populations grow in countries with scarce water or land. In Ethiopia today there is some famine even in years of good rain. The country made the news regularly in the seventies and eighties as large flows of refugees sought refuge from a devastating cycle of famine and civil war. At the end of 1993, nearly 230,000

Ethiopians lived outside the country, mostly in Sudan, and at least half a million were internally displaced. At 57 million, Ethiopia's population has more than doubled in the last four decades. And, based on current growth rates, the nation faces a colossal increase of 106 million during the next 40 years. It is almost impossible to imagine how Ethiopia could possibly feed so many more people. The country has some of the world's most severely eroded soils; much of its cropland lies on steep slopes, and its tree cover stands at a mere 3 percent. Many in Ethiopia's next generation will probably have to choose between emigration and starvation.[41]

When governments and development institutions build public works projects in an effort to solve problems of hunger and poverty, they force many people to move, turning them into "oustees." Oustees have to make way as residential and agricultural areas are flooded by dams, buildings or farms are devoured by roads, and shantytowns are razed to make way for coal-burning plants.

A World Bank study notes that public works projects now uproot more than 10 million "oustees" in the developing world every year, most of whom remain within their countries. During the past decade, an estimated 80-90 million people have been resettled as a result of infrastructure programs involving dam construction and urban and transportation development. Other sectors have relocated millions more. As expanding populations pursue economic growth in the future, they will likely feel the need to build at an even faster rate than in the past. Already this trend is well under way in parts of East Asia.[42]

In developing countries, the displacement toll of the approximately 300 large dams that enter into construction every year is estimated to be above four million people. Even as objections to these projects are raised on ecological, as well as humanitarian, grounds, ever-larger dams are designed. The Three Gorges Dam planned for China's Yangtse River, for example, will displace an estimated one million people, destroying priceless cultural sites in the process. The urban development and transportation programs started each year in developing countries are estimated to displace an additional six million people.[43]

The Indonesian government even has a development project with the sole designated purpose of population transfer. The goal is to reduce overcrowding. Between 1950 and 1974, the government resettled 664,000 people through its "transmigration" project, taking them off Indonesia's main island of Java. With the World Bank adding its support beginning in 1975, almost 3.5 million more people moved. The relocations took place despite warnings, which later proved accurate, that the soils on the islands of destination were too poor to support so many people, and that the social costs of the project would be high.[44]

Natural disasters also force people from their homes. Many Bangladeshis, for example, live on flood plains downstream from the Himalaya Mountains because they cannot afford land in safer areas. Seeking safety in India, many have left their country, one of the most densely populated on earth and a nation that suffers from frequent floods and natural disasters. Their migrations, which have touched off tensions between the two neighbors, are the result of acute land hunger.

Public works projects now uproot more than 10 million "oustees" in the developing world every year.

And as the region's population grows, larger numbers of people will live on the lands most susceptible to floods, hurricanes, and other disasters. That means that in the future each natural disaster will send a larger group of people looking for sustenance in other places. These people are eligible to receive some forms of emergency assistance, but not as refugees.[45]

Even health problems can be a major factor in migration. In the former Czechoslovakia, for instance, pollution and industrial hazards have dramatically raised rates of heart disease, cancer, respiratory failures, and birth defects, with the highest illness rates occurring in the districts with the most disturbed environments, namely, North Moravia, North and West Bohemia, and Central Slovakia. Life spans in different parts of the former Czechoslovakia vary by as much as five years. In the most unhealthful areas, divorce rates are also the highest, as are rates of crime and drug addiction; and "inner emigration," as the government has called relocations of people from polluted regions to cleaner parts of the country, occurs frequently.[46]

At least 5 percent of the population leaves the Kola Peninsula in the extreme north of Russia every year to escape the effects of pollution. The average male life expectancy there is 50 years, and lung cancer, lead poisoning, and emphysema are epidemic among the workers in the huge, antiquated nickel smelters and mines. Malformed hearts and bone-marrow defects afflict more than 25 percent of all babies. The rates of heart disease and cancer are eight times as high as those in Moscow, but virtually everyone smokes so it is impossible to say which illnesses are caused by what pathogen.[47]

Even the less polluted parts of Russia are showing similar profiles. Life expectancy for men is now 59 years nationwide, in part because of poor hospital service, social breakdown, and other causes, but also in part because of pollution, including a variety of new, "ecological" diseases that have been reported recently, such as Alopecia (sudden hair loss in children).[48]

In many parts of the world, people are on the move because new borders are being drawn as provinces receive national autonomy and larger states collapse. Eritrea has split off from Ethiopia; Yugoslavia has disintegrated; and Czechoslovakia has peacefully broken apart. Many people have left their homes to move into newly created states that they prefer, or to flee new states that they find unsafe.

In the countries of the former Soviet Union, the phenomenon of migration brought about by shifting borders can be seen in an extreme form. In the past, the Soviet regime had relocated many people to regions far from their homelands. For instance, almost 25 million Russians live outside Russia, dispersed throughout the old Soviet republics. In Estonia, 30 percent of the population is Russian; in Latvia, the figure is 38 percent. Some of these expatriates will choose to return to the country of their ethnic origin; others will remain where they are.[49]

In the crowded countries of West Africa, national governments are said to control the borders only during the day. People flow freely across them at night. This trend could become even more dynamic in the future if some states collapse, as journalist Robert Kaplan anticipates they will, particularly in West Africa. "The classificatory grid of nation-states is going to be replaced by a jagged-glass pattern of city-states, shanty-states, nebulous and anarchic regionalisms," writes Kaplan. Should he be right, then, in a sense, the ensuing upheaval will also create a new kind of migrant—people who did not move, but around whom the borders shifted, leaving them in a new nation or a new state. Or even in a new kind of entity, neither a nation or a state. People may move in many directions under those circumstances.[50]

> **Five percent of the population leaves the Kola Peninsula in the north of Russia every year.**

Understandably, the changing types of migration and different categories of refugees have altered the way some countries respond to requests for asylum. The United States has been a long-time passionate defender of the principle of "first asylum," which says that people may not be returned against their will to a country where they may be endangered. Surprised by the magnitude of today's still-growing flows of refugees, however, the United States and some other governments are now backing away from this principle. Most boat people from Haiti, for example, were not allowed into the United States in the early nineties, although many Cuban refugees were. The United States at the time felt it had less interest in accepting Haitians than it had in opposing the Castro regime in Cuba. And many European countries that once would have been more likely to help people leaving the totalitarian East now are besieged by Easterners whom they do not want.[51]

In large part, this change stems from the difference between the people who fled the persecution envisioned in the 1951 U.N. definition and today's refugees, who often escape from different problems and move in larger numbers. During the Cold War, western governments believed they had a vested interest in fighting persecution in Communist regimes in the former Soviet Union and China as well as certain dictatorships in Southeast Asia and elsewhere, and immigration policies were designed to serve this end. (Some 96 percent of the refugees admitted to the United States during the Reagan Administration came from Communist countries.) Today, however, western policymakers feel less threatened by the social, economic, and environmental problems that set many people in motion.[52]

Some of these pressures will escalate in the future. Overcrowding, along with land scarcity and other stresses associated with it, will increase as the world population expands by nearly 90 million every year. Pollution will become even more widespread as economic growth and industrialization arrive in parts of Asia and other continents that have lacked them. Water tables will continue to be drawn down far faster than they can replenish themselves in many countries; soils will continue to erode. And, like many before them, some people will react to these pressures in the future by leaving their homes. Thus, war and persecution are not the only immediate causes of displacement. They are joined by many others.[53]

Moving Up the Pay Scale

The large gap in income between the rich and the poor of the world is at the root of some of the largest population movements of all. Tens of millions of workers have moved from poorer countries to richer ones to take advantage of higher wages paid in stronger currencies. At the beginning of the nineties, 19 percent of Burkina Faso's workers, and 17 percent of Egypt's and Swaziland's, were employed outside their countries. Jordan exported 44 percent of its labor force. (See Table 5.) At the receiving end, in Qatar, some 92 percent of the work force is imported, 89 percent in the United Arab Emirates, 70 percent in Oman, 30 percent in Switzerland, 17 percent in the Gambia, and 14 percent in Malaysia.[54]

The gaps in income among the people of the world have been widening. While the poorest quintile in 1960 received 2.3 percent of global income, by 1991 that revenue share had fallen to 1.4 percent. The portion received by the richest quintile, on the other hand, rose from 70 percent to 85 percent. In 1960, the richest 20 percent received 30 times more income than the

TABLE 5

Nationals Abroad, Circa 1990

Country	Population	Percent of Population or of Labor Force Abroad
Jordan	400,000 ea	44.4 lf
Russia	25,290,000	21.1
Belarus	2,132,000	20.7
Tajikistan	1,043,000	19.7
Burkina Faso	900,000 ea	19.6 lf
Egypt	2,500,000 ea	16.8 lf
Swaziland	30,000 ea	16.7 lf
Azerbaijan	965,000	13.4
Kazakhstan	1,601,000	9.6
Portugal	900,000	8.6
Morocco	1,600,000	6.4
Greece	500,000	5.0
Algeria	280,000 ea	4.7 lf
Turkey	2,500,000	4.3
Colombia	1,300,000	3.9
Pakistan	1,200,000 ea	3.8 lf
Italy	600,000 ea	2.5 lf
Philippines	1,200,000	2.0
Bangladesh	634,000 ea	1.8 lf
Indonesia	800,000	1.0
S. Korea	231,000 ea	1.0 lf
Malaysia	110,000	0.6

Source: Peter Stalker, The Work of Strangers (Geneva: International Labour Organization, 1994).

Table Note: "ea" means economically active people only. "lf" means percent of labor force only.

poorest 20 percent. By 1991, they received 61 times more. If this widening disparity has the same effect in the future that it has had in the past, it will drive millions more from poor countries to richer ones in search of jobs.[55]

At the beginning of the 1990s, the poorest quintile of the

world population accounted for 0.9 percent of world trade, 1.1 percent of global domestic investment, 0.9 percent of global domestic savings, and 0.2 percent of global commercial credit. Each of those shares declined between 1960 and 1990. This means that the distribution of economic activity in the world is at least as skewed as the distribution of wealth, so it will be difficult for the poor to work to make up the difference. For some of them, this will leave few options other than migration.[56]

The gap in levels of economic activity has arisen and widened not only because of impoverishment, but sometimes also because of the success some regions of the world have in generating ever-larger amounts of wealth. As such, it is not entirely a negative trend. However, its unanticipated effects must be acknowledged, and migration is one of them.

Globally, the remittances of migrant workers—the money they earn abroad and then send home to their families and communities—are a crucial economic resource. By the end of the eighties, remittances amounted to more than $65 billion a year according to a World Bank study, second only to crude oil in their value to the world's economy, and larger than all official development assistance. Almost half of this money went to developing countries. Of course, these funds come at no small social cost to the families and communities that are split up when workers leave. And exportation of workers denies emigrants' countries the labor and skills of those individuals. Yet without remittances, many families and communities would be in desperate circumstances.[57]

In total, over 100 million people are thought to be living outside their countries in order to work or to be with family members who are working. The figure of 100 million, though, is an estimate based on census data from the mid-eighties, the most recent global migration data available. If better data were gathered, our understanding of migratory flows would improve, especially since recent trends probably have had major effects. With the breakup of the Soviet Union, for example, the number of migrants in the world has undoubtedly risen, because new countries were created that already had millions of (newly created) foreigners within their borders. Not only are some 25 million Russians living in former Soviet Republics but a similar number of nationals from these republics reside in Russia.[58]

The number of workers in poor countries in need of jobs will increase dramatically in the future. (See Table 6.) During the next two decades alone, the world's labor force is projected to grow by nearly a billion people. Most of these new workers will reside in the Third World, and few of their countries, even the ones that reach their goals for economic growth, are likely to be able to create adequate numbers of jobs for them. From 1975 to 1990, world economic production grew 56 percent, but world employment rose only 28 percent. By 2000, world production is projected to have more than doubled since 1975, but employment is expected to rise by less than half. In Mexico, one million new jobs will have to be created every year to match the rate at which young people are entering the work force; in Egypt, half a million jobs will be needed annually.[59]

The remittances of migrant workers amount to more than $65 billion a year, larger than all official development assistance.

The youthfulness of many countries virtually ensures that they will export labor in the future. More than 70 percent of Arabs have been born since 1970, and in Africa almost half the population has been born since 1980, which also holds true for Cambodia, Guatemala, Laos, and Nicaragua, and many other countries. As those children reach working age, they will need jobs somewhere. Unless their countries create or receive considerable investment in job-creating industries, many new workers will have to look abroad.[60]

Economic migrations are helped along by other factors as well. In some receiving countries, illegal migrants are actively recruited by employers because they will accept low wages and work for short periods of time without additional commitment, and because they will probably not demand retirement or health or other benefits. Some Americans believe that one of the reasons the United States receives so many migrants

TABLE 6

The Increasing Need for Employment, Developing Regions Only, 1950–2025

Year	Workers	Additional Jobs Needed
	(millions)	(millions)
1950	802	-
1960	916	114
1970	1,120	204
1980	1,416	296
1990	1,778	362
2000	2,138	360
2010	2,511	373
2020	2,863	352
2025	3,013	150

Source: Ignacy Sachs, "Population, development, and employment," International Social Science Journal, Population: Issues & Policies (Oxford: UNESCO and Basil Blackwell Publishers, September, 1994) and Worldwatch calculations.

from Latin America is that a major segment of the U.S. economy benefits from the presence of undocumented immigrants, and hence a lobby exists that wishes illegal immigration to continue. Without that desire, they say, management of the border would be less inept. But so long as it has a leaky border, the United States is in the enviable position of having a nearly limitless supply of inexpensive labor clamoring at its gates.[61]

This symbiotic relationship between American employers and Mexican workers goes back several decades. During the fifties and sixties the United States recruited 4.6 million Mexican farm workers. These green-card commuters were middle-aged by the mid-seventies, and their sons began to replace them in U.S. fields where employers faced no penalties for hiring "illegals." European countries also imported labor. During the sixties, a time of economic growth, labor shortages in northern Europe created widespread vacancies in the job markets of Germany, France, and other countries. To sustain the economic boom, these nations recruited guestworkers from Italy, Turkey, and Algeria.[62]

Once in Northern Europe, those workers became part of networks abroad that would welcome future arrivals from their original countries—this social infrastructure of migration has usually sprung up wherever significant numbers of immigrants congregated. Most migrants rely on family members or friends already settled in their destination countries to help them adjust and find work, and a strong correlation exists between the choices of destination of emigrants and the locations of their friends and families.[63]

Much migration in quest of jobs is from countryside to city. In 1970, a quarter of the developing world's population lived in cities; by 2025, at least 57 percent will be urban, if U.N. projections prove correct. (See Table 7.) In industrial countries, the urban population will have risen from 67 percent to 84 percent in that same time. Right now there are 143,000 people per square mile in Lagos, Nigeria, and 130,000 per square mile in Jakarta, Indonesia, as compared with only 23,700 per square mile in the five boroughs of New York city. One daring projection found that about 15 years from now the rural population of the Third World will begin to decrease—despite rapid overall population growth—while urban populations keep growing. Some of that growth will come from children born in cities, but its size is also a testament to the combined pull of opportunity (or perceived opportunity) in urban areas and the push of poverty in rural areas.[64]

Once in a city, many of these migrants live in squatter settlements with open sewers that run through the middle of the streets where children play; their homes are cardboard or sheet metal shacks, where families are crowded into one room; disease runs rampant. These cities then become international jumping-off points for migration by people trying to escape difficult living conditions. It is here that shady "travel agencies" take people's last savings in exchange for clandestine passages across national borders. For Chinese migrants, a highly specialized black market exists to move them to Eastern Europe, North America, Australia, and elsewhere.[65]

TABLE 7

Share of Population Living in Urban Areas, by Region, 1970 and 1990, with Projections to 2025

Region	1970	1990	2025
		(percent)	
Africa	23	32	54
Asia (excl. Japan)	20	29	54
Latin America	57	72	84
Europe	67	73	85
North America	74	75	85
World	37	43	61

Source: United Nations, World Urbanization Prospects, 1992 Revision (New York: 1993).

The rise in already large income disparities between urban and rural areas is responsible in part for the growth of cities. Despite the recent resumption of economic growth in Latin America, U.N. economists say that no progress is expected in reducing poverty, which by their calculations is even likely to increase slightly. This is because so much of the new income goes to people who are already well-to-do—in a continent that already has some of the world's widest income disparities. Since this situation is unlikely to change in the foreseeable future, impoverished country people will continue to be drawn to the locus of jobs, even though they will be paid relatively little. Thus it is not entirely a coincidence that Latin America is by far the most urbanized region of the developing world. From 1950 to today, city dwellers there have risen from 42 percent of the population to 73 percent.[66]

For some years, China has experienced some of the most equal distribution of income in the world. Now, however, that is changing as incomes in its southern provinces and special economic zones soar while those in rural areas rise much more slowly. The poor have suffered from price increases without benefitting from the additional income in the country. The Chinese government now counts more than 100 million "surplus farm laborers" who have migrated to the cities and special economic zones, and every year another 15 million are added. While unequal income distribution plays a role in this shift, other, universal spurs to rural-urban migration must be noted, especially the inroads of mechanization, the desire of rural workers to escape grueling work, and the enticement of what appear to be bright prospects in cities.[67]

The government of China has tried to stop the migration to cities, imposing a tax of up to $11,600 for the privilege of living in Beijing, for example—a prohibitive amount by rural standards—but the tax and other, similar measures are unenforceable. No government measure has been able to overcome the pull of the astonishing growth of income in the special economic zones and the coastal regions, where expansion is so high that it has ratcheted up the GDP of the entire country by a remarkable 10-12 percent during most recent years. The Chinese Academy of Social Sciences says that by 2010, half the population will live in cities, compared with 28 percent today and only 10 percent in the early eighties.[68]

The Chinese government now counts more than 100 million "surplus farm laborers."

Meanwhile, in some regions almost no one is getting richer. The per capita income of most sub-Saharan African nations actually fell during the eighties. After the latest negotiations of the General Agreement on Tariffs and Trade (GATT) were completed, the *Wall Street Journal* reported that "even GATT's most energetic backers say that in one part of the world, the trade accord may do more harm than good: sub-Saharan Africa," the poorest region on the globe.[69]

In Africa, an estimated one-third of all college graduates have left the continent. That loss of talented people, due in large part to poverty and a lack of opportunities in Africa, will make it even more difficult for the continent to grow richer and to generate opportunities for its peoples in the future. Thus economic conditions contribute to migration, and migration in turn affects economic conditions, creating a cycle that has been cruel not just to Africa, but to many parts of the planet.[70]

Following the Money

In certain areas around the world, economic conditions have either slowed migration or reversed it. South Korea, Hong Kong, Singapore, Taiwan, and Malaysia are all countries whose citizens once went abroad to start new lives—and often faced discrimination there—but which now find themselves (often unwilling) hosts to significant numbers of foreign workers. Thus, economic growth can have the potential to reverse emigration, though only in the long run.[71]

Indeed, many economic trends affect migration. Technologies that change the structure of the labor force can create more emigrants, for example, by reducing the need for certain kinds of labor and causing unemployment. And people often emigrate to nations with histories of private investment in their country of origin because they have already been introduced to those cultures, languages, and economic systems. Hence, foreign investment plays a role both in the decisions of workers to migrate and in their choices of destination.[72]

International trade also affects the migration of workers, whether they travel overseas as part of commerce or the production of goods, or remain home to work in jobs created by export-based economic growth. Most commonly, the following scenario is played out. In the short term, trade increases migration. Policies associated with free trade and economic reform—including privatization, strict monetary policies, and elimination of barriers to the transport of goods—produce a "hump" of increased emigration. They disrupt past livelihoods and create new ones, sending people abroad looking for different work. Under the North American Free Trade Agreement (NAFTA), for example, the Mexican corn sector will be hit hard because U.S. production is more efficient, its yields far higher. Some of the workers who lose jobs in Mexico will go to sectors of the Mexican

economy where NAFTA gives an advantage to Mexican prod-
ucts. Others, however, will feel the need to emigrate from Mexico.
In the long run, though, the desired economic growth (if it
comes) will settle people into solid, long-
term jobs in their home regions, reducing migration.[73]

South Korea has

The movement of people as workers is **become an**
integral to ideas of international trade. **importer, rather**
But it is not an easy movement: Adam
Smith once asserted that "man is of all **than an exporter,**
sorts of luggage the most difficult to be **of labor.**
transported." Most economic goods—cap-
ital, assembly, knowledge, management—have become global-
ized, moving across national boundaries in the form of investments, consulting expertise, new plants, patents, and so on.
But national governments have tried to keep one good, labor,
exempt from that globalization by limiting its flow. Among
economic goods, it is the odd factor out.[74]

In East and Southeast Asia, labor migration is increasing
rapidly as these regions continue to experience dynamic economic growth. It could be years before these migrants settle
down, if they ever do so. South Korea is ahead of most of the
pack, and its experience gives insight. The country sent more
workers out as it industrialized in the 1980s than it did during
the 1970s, before industrialization. But now it has become an
importer, rather than an exporter, of labor. Likewise, the 48
million Europeans who emigrated during Europe's industrialization between 1850 and 1925 constituted about one-eighth of
Europe's population in 1900, so emigration was common during Europe's industrialization and commercial expansion. But
that emigration slowed after those countries became wealthier,
and now they are countries of immigration instead. Italy and
Germany, for example, have gone through this cycle.[75]

These trends create a dilemma for a country like the United
States, which wants to use NAFTA to reduce migration from
Mexico. The strategy is plausible, but it will take years to have
an effect. Indeed, in the short run it might add to border cross-
ings. According to Philip Martin of the University of California

at Davis, with 20 to 50 percent of Mexico's farmers projected to leave the land over the next decade, the stage is set for a repeat of a great migration similar to that in the United States in the 1950s and 1960s when U.S. sharecroppers left the South. This would generate a small but significant increase in Mexican immigration into the United States in the short run. In the long run, as happened in the past with Italy and Spain, emigration would slow. Thus, long- and short-run effects are quite different.[76]

But the "hump" scenario is not guaranteed. With extensive networks of Mexicans in the United States, for example, heavy emigration could continue even with sound economic growth in Mexico, for other reasons. Such has been, at least in part, the case with Puerto Ricans moving to the United States, and Turks moving to Europe. Many other such factors could intervene to prevent the hump from rising, or from falling.[77]

Because of the extent of trade and international investment, economic events on one side of the world can pull the floor out from under people thousands of miles away. For example, changes in European or North American markets in the price of soybeans or coffee have led people to vacate their homes in South America and Africa. In the late seventies, coffee prices fell in markets around the world. In Brazil, a major coffee producer, farmers switched to different crops, especially soybeans. But coffee production is particularly labor intensive, and soybean production much less so. As a result, unemployment rose, giving rise to a stream of migrants who moved into the frontier areas of uncut forests in the interior. (This massive migration was exacerbated, to be sure, by one of the most unequal land distribution systems in the world.)[78]

Shifts in the gold markets had a similar impact in the late seventies, when gold prices rose sharply, and gold mining in Brazil took off. Tens of thousands of landless workers left low-paying jobs in the coastal areas to move inland and prospect for the metal. They cleared virgin lands, opened large pits, and often forced out indigenous peoples, some of whom then had no choice but to migrate themselves.[79]

Countries that follow an export-oriented path often experience unequal growth, in which small segments of their society who own capital and industries earn considerable income but the remainder benefit much less. The resulting inequitable distribution of income can itself contribute to migration, in this case within a country.[80]

One modern attempt to lessen poverty involves the structural adjustment programs of the International Monetary Fund and World Bank, which seek to put a country's economy in good order by setting up strict policies regarding the money supplies, exchange rates, trade, and other economic matters in countries that have borrowed large amounts of money. Much debate rages over the success or failure of these programs in the long run. In the short run, however, these measures can worsen poverty and thus affect migration. When Poland had its first experience with such economic shock therapy in 1990, for example, inflation hit 240 percent and 1.3 million people lost their jobs. Tens of thousands abandoned the country. Other East European countries have faced similar shocks. Cuts in social expenditures for government subsidies on food, education, health care, and home heating fuel—which are also required by the adjustment policy—fall most heavily on the poor and lead many to move.[81]

Research by the World Resources Institute on the effects of a structural adjustment program in the Philippines found that the program worsened short-term poverty in urban areas by cutting social expenditures. That led to an urban-to-rural migration to upland regions and coastal areas as people sought livelihoods from the fields, fisheries, and forests outside Manila and other cities.[82]

An economic liberalization program in Sri Lanka beginning in the late seventies cut social programs and increased emphasis on export industries, resulting in declining real wages, food insecurity for the lowest income group, deterioration of the social welfare system, and widening income disparities. The authors of one report argue that much of the movement of Sri Lankans to the Persian Gulf was a case of "survival migration" by those in the poorest strata of society, mostly women who went to work as domestic servants.[83]

The short-term contribution of adjustment programs to unwanted emigration poses a serious dilemma because such programs are needed to combat the high inflation and financial chaos that also can cause people to leave. Without adjustment, in some cases emigration will still occur, but for different reasons—because economies are completely out of control. The beginnings of a solution might come if the economists who plan adjustment programs took migration into account during their work by forecasting movements of people. They could then at least consider the possibility of altering programs when emigration appears too severe.

As it is, with many economic policies and programs, migration is an afterthought. A few take it into account, as President Clinton's promotion of the NAFTA agreement did. But most economic thinking is done without considering the effects of various actions on population movement. If countries choose to make migration a topic of highest importance, then they will want to consider it more fully when they make their economic plans.

Defusing the Pressures

Without actions that enhance the stability of countries and the security of individuals, we face a future of widespread and growing population movement. But understanding its complex origins will put us in a position to reduce involuntary migration and flight.

Finding and implementing such solutions will depend on expanding the way we now think about security. As U.N. Secretary-General Boutros Boutros-Ghali observed, "territorial security has been largely guaranteed, but human security is in crisis." A survey of the world's wars today bears him out. Although there may be only one war between two countries at any given moment, almost a billion people face food insecurity.[84]

It follows that a new notion of security is needed, one in which economic development and environmental protection play a central part. Already, several developing countries are beginning to demonstrate that long-term development programs that target the poor and address social concerns like education and hunger and public health make people more resilient and thus better able to weather difficulties that would otherwise force them out of their communities.

Along these lines, newly independent Eritrea has embarked on an experiment that could eventually become a model for other countries in the future. This war-ravaged country is deliberately avoiding the mistakes—such as over-reliance on large-scale public works projects and heavy borrowing of foreign funds—that typified past development thinking.[85]

Instead of selecting the large schemes that are common in many development programs, Eritrea is placing emphasis on small-scale rehabilitation of lands and communities broken up by war, and on peasant agriculture. The government intends to ward off future droughts and famine by beginning irrigation and soil protection projects today. Land redistribution is designed to give farmers a stake in protecting their soil and to ensure that as many members of society as possible receive adequate incomes. Programs to demobilize soldiers and repatriate refugees include training and finance to help them participate in business projects with pooled resources. New roads, schools, clinics, and telecommunications are being built to strengthen rural economies so that inhabitants are not driven to migrate to cities in order to support their families.[86]

Although there may be only one war between two countries at any given moment, almost a billion people face food insecurity.

In Bangladesh, one of the most densely populated countries on earth, tiny sums of a few dollars lent to poor villagers by the locally organized Grameen Bank have enabled people in the poorest class to generate viable income. Such efforts should be recognized for their ability to enhance security by making societies more resilient.[87]

Recently in neighboring India, government officials tacitly endorsed such development, dropping their short-term view of immigration in favor of a response that has the potential to work more effectively in the long term. Instead of just continuing to support a crackdown on Bangladeshi migrants into the Indian state of Assam, they now endorse economic development across the border. "The only way to stop people from leaving Bangladesh is to improve conditions there," explained an Indian diplomat who works on migration issues between the two countries.[88]

Likewise in Thailand, distribution of income to rural areas is a government policy intended to keep people in rural provinces and curb mass migration to Bangkok. A clutch of companies taking part in the "Thai Business Initiative in Rural Development," for example, (run by the Population and Community Development Association, Thailand's largest non-governmental organization) are creating jobs in rural areas. There people set up small factories, producing silk, glass, shoes, protective gear, brooms. They are helped by private companies, many of which are European and North American. The scale of the program is still small, but it is growing and is expected to involve about 500 companies by 1996, many of them employing hundreds of people.[89]

Nearby, the Indonesian government has created a program, called "Inpres Desa Tertinggal" (IDT), that allots money directly to groups of 30 or so villagers to be used as initial capital for income-generating projects. The villagers make their own collective decisions on how to spend the funds, although all proposals must be approved by local governments. IDT field workers are on hand to assist the villagers. So far, payback rates on the loans are higher than on those from commercial banks. For the most part, the program seems to be succeeding in getting income to the poorest Indonesians.[90]

Bolivia has decided to overhaul the distribution of benefits from its government in order to increase the resources going to its Inca and Aymara citizens, who comprise 70 percent of the total population. Rural communities will now have the authority to decide what to do with 20 percent of the national budget, up from 9 percent in 1993. Other changes include allowing local Indian dialects to be used in schools, and freeing poor Indians who are currently in jail because of unpaid debts. The avoidance of social conflict and mass migration to cities is an express goal of the program. "If this nation didn't come up with such proposals," said one government official, "it could soon find itself facing a Chiapas or a Shining Path." All of these are examples of programs that will enhance people's security, helping them to avoid destabilizing pressures.[91]

Many initiatives not normally considered relevant to refugee or migration policy are actually central to giving people the security they need to remain at home. The International Conference on Population and Development held in Cairo in September 1994 was one such effort. Its plan to keep world population below 9.8 billion people by the year 2050 by focusing on such needs as literacy for women, health care, and family planning directly addresses the sources of some of the insecurities and poverty and wars that force people out of their homes. Likewise, UNICEF's recent success in innoculating infants around the world—over the last decade, three million children have been saved by immunizations every year—is a significant contribution to stability. Families that have healthy children tend to have fewer of them and are able to make larger investments in the education and care of their offspring. Healthy, educated children are one cornerstone of secure societies.[92]

Such endeavors of governments and international institutions working with local leaders may lack the dramatic appeal (and immediate economic impact) of large dams or nuclear power plants, but they do help avoid the future conflicts and destitution that lead to displacement of people. And they are often less disruptive to the environment and to societies than huge public works projects.

If problems like illiteracy seem far removed from the pressures that turn people into refugees, the fact that no democracy with a relatively free press has ever suffered a major famine suggests otherwise. In the past, people who have had access to information have foreseen the famines and prevented them with imports of food. If access by literate people to public debate seems only tenuously related to warfare to be relevant, the fact that no two democracies have ever gone to war against each other strongly hints at a connection.[93]

Unfortunately, just as crisis-driven expenditures are rising in response to increased flows of migrants and refugees, efforts to attack the underlying causes of flight are decreasing. Official development assistance from the world's 25 wealthiest countries fell by 8 percent in 1993. In 1994, the United Nations expected to spend at least $1 billion more on refugees and peace-keeping than on economic development. The current budget of the U.N. Development Programme is not much larger than that of the U.N. High Commission for Refugees.[94]

The urgency of shifting current views on the nature of migration is underscored by the likelihood that some countries that are not sources of refugees today will become so during the next few years. The United Nations recently voiced particularly strong concern about Angola, Iraq, Myanmar (formerly Burma), and Sudan. Zaire has collapsed politically and economically, and is expected to encounter increasing insecurity in the future. Nigeria's elected government has been kept out of office by the military, and violent clashes have resulted, raising the possibility of a flight from that country.[95]

As we enter a future where pressures of land scarcity, demographic change, environmental degradation, and other sources of conflict are intensifying, the creation of organizations designed to defuse the tensions exacerbated by these stresses will sound increasingly plausible and necessary. Such organizations will be needed in parts of the world now lacking them, and they should be given long-term mandates for avoiding crises. Inspiration for this approach lies in existing security mechanisms like the Conference on Security and Cooperation in Europe, which helped to calm that continent's arguments over economic and security issues in the eighties. In the future, these groups will be called on to try to reduce other kinds of tensions.

Rather than wait until the cumulative pressures that drive people from their homes get out of hand, people concerned about excessive migration can take specific action. Where land scarcity threatens to cause hunger or joblessness and makes people insecure, it is land security that must be addressed, rather than the departures that are symptoms of the insecurity.

Investments in agricultural productivity—fertilizers, irrigation wells, research on appropriate crops, and careful soil management and education of farmers—can help accomplish that. Where disease rates are leading to large numbers of broken families, public health and education campaigns can head off some of those tragedies—if they start early. Such an approach offers an alternative to the sense of hopelessness that currently prevails.

Fortunately, we do not have to achieve perfect stability. Many countries are able to absorb refugees and immigrants, and many countries need the labor and vibrancy they provide. Especially if intolerance toward foreigners can be reduced, many countries will continue to benefit from newcomers in myriad ways. The goal should be to improve stability in all regions so that people who want to remain home can do so.

Notes

1. Migrant figure is a Worldwatch estimate based on United Nations, "International Migration Stock, Trends In Total Migrant Stock," (electronic database), United Nations, New York, 1994, and on Hania Zlotnik, Population Division, United Nations, private communication, October 3, 1994; Refugee figures from United Nations High Commission for Refugees (UNHCR), Washington, D.C., private communication, February 10, 1995; Spanish migration from Aaron Segal, *An Atlas of International Migration* (London: Hans Zell Publishers, 1993).

2. Rwanda information from Tina Malone, Catholic Relief Services, Baltimore, Md., private communication, September 22, 1994; Chinese water scarcity and migration from Frederick W. Crook, *Agricultural Statistics of the People's Republic of China, 1949-86* (Washington, D.C.: U.S. Department of Agriculture [USDA], Economic Research Service [ERS], 1988) and Nie Lisheng, "State Organizes Farmers to Work on Irrigation," *China Daily*, January 16, 1988, and from World Bank, *China: Strategies for Reducing Poverty in the 1990s* (Washington, D.C.: World Bank, 1992).

3. World Bank, op. cit. note 2; Paul Theroux, "Going to See the Dragon," *Harpers Magazine*, October 1993.

4. Mike Edwards, "Chornobyl [sic]: Living With the Monster," *National Geographic*, August 1994.

5. Population Reference Bureau (PRB), *1994 World Population Data Sheet* (Washington, D.C.: 1994); USDA, "Production, Supply, and Demand View" (electronic database), Washington, D.C., November 1993.

6. Robert M. Press, "UN Plans Somalia Exit; Warlords Still Battle: West missed war over farmland, analysts say," *Christian Science Monitor*, October 18, 1994; Bruce Byers, "Roots of Somalia's Crisis," *Christian Science Monitor*, December 24, 1992; U.S. Committee for Refugees, *1994 World Refugee Survey* (Washington, D.C.: USCR, 1994).

7. Victor Mallet, "Vietnamese Settlers in Cambodia Flee Attacks," *Financial Times*, March 31, 1993.

8. Population density from PRB, op. cit. note 5; "Rwanda: A Case of Successful Adaptation," in World Bank, *Sub-Saharan Africa: From Crisis to Sustainable Growth* (Washington, D.C.: 1989); farm size from Centro Internacional de Agricultura Tropical, "Rwanda Civil War Disrupts Key African Food Program," *CIAT On-Line: News on Research Progress, Impact, and Achievement*, July 1994.

9. Number of refugees from U.S. Agency for International Development, "Consolidated Rwanda Report, Update #10," August 30-September 8, 1994.

10. Tina Malone, op. cit. note 2.

11. Benoit Bosquet, Africa Department, World Bank, Washington, D.C., private communication, July 19, 1994; Malone, op. cit. note 2; Diana Johnstone, "Africa: Making a Killing," *In These Times*, December 26, 1994.

12. Malone, op. cit. note 2; PRB, op. cit. note 5.

13. Thomas L. Friedman, *From Beirut to Jerusalem* (New York: Anchor Books, 1989).

14. Ibid.

15. Kenyan cropland scarcity from United Nations, *Report on the World Social Situation 1993* (New York: 1993); Keith B. Richburg, "Kenya's Ethnic Conflict Drives Farmers Off Land," *Washington Post,* March 17, 1994; Leslie Crawford, "Suffering the Politics of Drought," *Financial Times,* March 17, 1994; Tribal Clashes Resettlement Volunteer Service, "Politically Motivated Tribal Clashes in Kenya," Nairobi, Kenya: undated; doubling time from PRB, op. cit. note 5.

16. Jack A. Goldstone, *Revolution and Rebellion in the Early Modern World* (Berkeley: University of California Press, 1991).

17. Ibid.

18. UNHCR, op. cit. note 1; UNHCR, *The State of the World's Refugees 1993: The Challenge of Protection* (London: Penguin, 1993); Rosemarie Rogers and Emily Copeland, *Forced Migration: Policy Issues in the Post-Cold War World* (Medford, Mass: The Fletcher School of Law and Diplomacy, 1993); Gil Loescher, *Beyond Charity* (Oxford: Oxford University Press, 1993).

19. Worldwatch calculation based on UNHCR, op. cit. note 1, and on data from Milton Leitenberg and Nicole Ball, "Appendix I. Wars and Conflicts in Developing Economies and Estimates of Related deaths since the End of World War II," in Robert S. McNamara, "The Post-Cold War World: Implications for Military Expenditure in the Developing Countries," *Proceedings of the World Bank Annual Conference on Development Economics 1991* (Washington, D.C.: World Bank, 1992).

20. Ibid.

21. Peter Wallensteen and Karin Axell, "Conflict Resolution and the End of the Cold War, 1989-93," in Ylva Nordlander (ed.), *States in Armed Conflict 1993,* Report No. 38, Department of Peace and Conflict Research, Uppsala University, Sweden; Ruth Leger Sivard, *World Military and Social Expenditures 1993* (Washington, D.C.: World Priorities, 1993); Leitenberg and Ball, op. cit. note 19; data for 1994 are Worldwatch estimates based on newspaper reports during 1994.

22. Worldwatch calculation based on data from Leitenberg and Ball, op. cit. note 19, and on data from Wallensteen and Axell, op. cit. note 21.

23. Michael Renner, *Critical Juncture: The Future of Peacekeeping,* Worldwatch Paper 114 (Washington, D.C.: Worldwatch Institute, May 1993); Barbara Crossette, "Unicef Optimistic About Saving More Children from Disease," *New York Times,* December 16, 1994; Lois Whitman and Janet Fleischman, "The Child Soldiers," *Africa Report,* July/August 1994.

24. Worldwatch calculation based on data from Leitenberg and Ball, op. cit. note 19, and Wallensteen and Axell, op. cit. note 21; UNHCR, op. cit. note 1.

25. Project Ploughshares, Institute of Peace and Conflict Studies, Conrad Grebel College, Armed Conflicts Report 1993 (Waterloo, Ontario: Project Ploughshares, October 1994).

26. Ibid.

27. Ian Steele, "Countries Prepare for War While People Die of Hunger, Disease," *Depthnews Asia*, June, 1994; United Nations Development Programme (UNDP), *Human Development Report 1994* (New York: Oxford University Press, 1994).

28. UNHCR, *The State of the World's Refugees*, op. cit. note 18.

29. Machiavelli quote from Christa Meindsma, quoted in "UN Recognizes Population Transfer as a Violation of Human Rights," *Tibet Press Watch*, December 1992; Department of Information and International Relations, Central Tibetan Administration of His Holiness the XIV Dalai Lama, "Tibet: Environment and Development Issues 1992," Dharamsala, India, 1992; International Campaign for Tibet, "The Long March: Chinese Settlers and Chinese Policies in Eastern Tibet, Results of a Fact Finding Mission in Tibet," Dharamsala, India, September 1991.

30. Iraqi exodus cited in Raymond Bonner, "Trail of Suffering as Rwandan Exodus Continues," *New York Times*, July 16, 1994.

31. UNHCR, op. cit. note 1.

32. Worldwatch calculations based on data from Leitenberg and Ball, op. cit. note 19, and on data from Wallensteen and Axell, op. cit. note 21; UNHCR, op. cit. note 1; Howard W. French, "Liberia's War Refugees Now United in Misery," *New York Times*, September 17, 1994.

33. Jim Wurst, "Mozambique Disarms," *The Bulletin of the Atomic Scientists*, September/October, 1994; Dan Connell, "Eritrea: An island of stability in strife-filled Africa," *Christian Science Monitor*, November 30, 1994; Judith Matloff, "Angola Edges Toward Cease-Fire As UN Brokers New Peace Accord," *Christian Science Monitor*, October 21, 1994; Wallensteen and Axell, op. cit. note 21.

34. UNHCR, op. cit. note 1.

35. Worldwatch calculations based on data from Leitenberg and Ball, op. cit. note 21, and on data from Wallensteen and Axell, op. cit. note 22.

36. New wars started in Haiti and the Chechnyan province of the Russian Federation; wars that ended or showed some signs of ending include those in Haiti, Peru, South Africa, Angola, Rwanda (maybe), Israel (peace with Jordan and limited Palestinian self-rule), and Northern Ireland. Source: Worldwatch calculations based on newspaper reports during 1994 and 1995.

37. U.S. Committee for Refugees (USCR), *World Refugee Survey* 1994 (Washington, D.C.: 1994).

38. UNHCR, op. cit. note 1.

39. Worldwatch estimate based on Hania Zlotnik, Population Division, United Nations, private communication, October 3, 1994; on Michael S. Teitelbaum, Sloan Foundation, private communication, October 3, 1993; and on Segal, op. cit. note 1.

40. The Population Institute, "Desperate Departures: The Flight of Environmental Refugees," a special report of the Population Institute for the U.N. Expert Group Meeting on Population, Distribution, and Migration, 18-22 January, 1993, in Santa Cruz, Bolivia (Washington, D.C.: Population Institute, 1992); Sadruddin Aga Khan, "Stemming the Flow," *Our Planet,* the United Nations Environment Programme Magazine for Sustainable Development, Volume 6 Number 5, 1994.

41. USDA, "Production, Supply, and Demand View" (electronic database), Washington, D.C., November 1993; population figures from U.S. Bureau of the Census, published in Francis Urban and Ray Nightingale, *World Population by Country and Region, 1950-90 and Projections to 2050* (Washington, D.C.: USDA, ERS, 1993); USCR, op. cit. note 37.

42. World Bank Environment Department, *Resettlement and Development: The Bankwide Review of Projects Involving Involuntary Resettlement 1986-1993* (Washington, D.C.: 1994).

43. Ibid; Joseph Kahn, "Dammed Yangtze: Despite Vast Obstacles, Chinese Move to Tap Power of Historic River," *New York Times,* April 18, 1994.

44. Bruce Rich, *Mortgaging the Earth* (Boston: Beacon Press, 1994).

45. Sanjoy Hazarika, "Bangladesh and Assam: Land Pressures, Migration and Ethnic Conflict," *Occasional Paper Series* of the Project on Environmental Change and Acute Conflict of the International Security Studies Program of the American Academy of Arts and Sciences and the Peace and Conflict Studies Program of the University of Toronto, Number 3, March 1993.

46. Josef Vavrousek and Colleagues, Department of the Environment, State Commission for Science, Technology, and Investments, *The Environment in Czechoslovakia* (Prague: Institute of Technical, Economic, and Ecological Information, 1990).

47. Michael Specter, "Far North in Russia, the Mines' Fatal Blight," *New York Times,* March 28, 1994.

48. Boris Revich, Center for Demography and Human Ecology, "Incidence of New 'Ecological' Diseases Noted," *Environmental Issues JPRS-Ten,* May 5, 1992; Russian life expectancy from Carl Haub, "Former USSR Shaken by Dramatic Demographic Changes, *Press Release,* PRB, Washington, D.C., January 10, 1995.

49. Jaques Attali, "An Age of Yugoslavias," *Harpers Magazine,* January 1993 (reprinted from *New Perspectives Quarterly,* Fall 1992).

50. Robert D. Kaplan, "The Coming Anarchy," *The Atlantic Monthly,* February 1994.

51. Morton Abramowitz, "Exodus: The World Refugee Crisis," *Foreign Policy,* Summer 1994.

52. Ibid.; refugees admitted to United States during Reagan years from Loescher, op. cit. note 18.

53. Population figures from U.S. Bureau of the Census, published in Francis Urban and Ray Nightingale, op. cit. note 41.

54. Segal, op. cit. note 1; Peter Stalker, *The Work of Strangers* (Geneva: International Labour Organization, 1994).

55. UNDP, *Human Development Report 1994* (New York and Oxford: Oxford University Press, 1994).

56. UNDP, *Human Development Report 1993* (New York and Oxford: Oxford University Press, 1993).

57. Sharon Stanton Russell and Michael S. Teitelbaum, "International Migration and International Trade," *World Bank Discussion Paper 160* (Washington, D.C.: World Bank, 1992).

58. Worldwatch estimates based on data from United Nations, op. cit. note 1.

59. UNDP, op. cit. note 55; Emma Tucker, "Global Pressures Are Getting Worse," *Financial Times,* January 31, 1994.

60. Arab youthfulness from Kaplan, op. cit. note 50; All others from PRB, op. cit. note 5.

61. Maxine L. Margolis, Professor of Anthropology, University of Florida, "Immigration Chaos Keeps U.S. in Cheap Labor," letter to the editor, *New York Times,* September 9, 1994.

62. Philip L. Martin, *Trade and Migration: NAFTA and Agriculture* (Washington, D.C.: Institute for International Economics, October 1993).

63. Ibid.

64. United Nations, *Prospects of World Urbanization 1988* (New York: 1989); Matthew Connelly and Paul Kennedy, "Must It Be the Rest Against the West?" *The Atlantic Monthly,* December 1994; Jane Pryer and Nigel Crook, *Cities of Hunger: Urban Malnutrition in Developing Countries* (Oxford: Oxfam, 1988).

65. Jorge E. Hardoy and David Satterthwaite, *Squatter Citizen* (London: Earthscan, 1989); Segal, op. cit. note 1; Roberto Suro, "Chinese Smuggling Grows, Forcing U.S. Resentment," *Washington Post,* June 2, 1994; Ashley Dunn, "Golden Venture, Then a New Ordeal," *New York Times,* June 5, 1994.

66. "Latin American Speedup Leaves Poor Behind," *New York Times,* September 7, 1994; Thomas Kamm, "Epidemic of Slums Afflicts Latin America," *Wall Street Journal,* August 30, 1994; United Nations, *World Urbanization Prospects, The 1992 Revision* (New York: United Nations, 1993).

67. World Bank, op. cit. note 2.

68. City tax from Patrick E. Tyler, "Beijing To Impose Huge Fees to Limit Migrants in City," *New York Times,* September 15, 1994; World Bank, op. cit. note 8; Tony Walker, "China's Golden Era 'To Last Well Into Next Century'," *Financial Times,* August 26, 1994; National Academy findings from "China's Next Revolution," *Financial Times,* August 26, 1994.

69. Helene Cooper, "Sub-Saharan Africa Is Seen as Big Loser in GATT's New World Trade Accord," *Wall Street Journal,* August 15, 1994.

70. Brain drain from John Darnton, "'Lost Decade' Drains Africa's Vitality,"

New York Times, June 19, 1994.

71. "The Rise of the Fortress NIC" *Development Hotline,* December 1993.

72. Peter Stalker, *The Work of Strangers: A Survey of International Labour Migration* (Geneva: International Labour Office, 1994).

73. Philip Martin, op. cit. note 62; Georges Photios Tapinos, Institut D'etudes Politiques de Paris, "International Migration and Development," *Population Bulletin of the United Nations 1994* (New York and Geneva: United Nations, 1994).

74. Georges Photios Tapinos, op. cit. note 73; Matthew Connelly and Paul Kennedy, op. cit. note 64.

75. Philip Martin, op. cit. note 62.

76 Ibid.

77. Ibid.

78. International Monetary Fund (IMF), *International Financial Statistics* (Washington, D.C.: various years); Ralph Hakkert and Franklin W. Goza, "The Demographic Consequences of Austerity in Latin America," in William L. Canak (ed.), *Lost Promises: Debt, Austerity, and Development in Latin America* (Boulder, Colo.: Westview Press, 1989).

79. Ibid.

80. UNDP, op. cit. note 55.

81. "Expert Group Meeting on Population Distribution and Migration," *Population Bulletin of the United Nations,* Nos. 34/35, 1993 (summary findings of The Expert Group Meeting held in Santa Cruz, Bolivia, 18-22 January 1993); Robin Wright and Doyle McManus, *Flashpoints: Promise and Peril in a New World* (New York: Alfred A. Knopf, 1991).

82. Wilfredo Cruz and Robert Repetto, *The Environmental Effects of Stabilization and Structural Adjustment Programs: The Philippines Case* (Washington, D.C.: World Resources Institute, 1992); Hakkert and Goza, op. cit. note 78.

83. Sharon Stanton Russell, review of *Labour Migration to the Middle East: From Sri Lanka to the Gulf, Population and Development Review,* September 1993.

84. Boutros-Ghali quote from R. Jeffrey Smith, "Demand for Humanitarian Aid May Skyrocket," *Washington Post,* December 17, 1994; war data Worldwatch calculation based on Wallensteen and Axell, op. cit. note 21; Hunger figure from United Nations Administrative Committee on Coordination—Subcommittee on Nutrition, *Second Report on the World Nutrition Situation, Volume I: Global and Regional Results (*Geneva: United Nations, October 1992).

85. Dan Connell, "The greening of Eritrea: famine unlikely to recur," *Christian Science Monitor,* November 30, 1994.

86. Ibid.

87. Andreas Fuglesang and Dale Chandler, *Participation As Process: What We Can*

Learn from Grameen Bank, Bangladesh (Dhaka, Bangladesh: Grameen Bank, 1988).

88. Sanjoy Hazarika, "India Weighs New Approach to Immigration," *New York Times,* February 12, 1995.

89. Rodney Tasker, "Home-Town Jobs," *Far Eastern Economic Review,* April 14, 1994.

90. Margot Cohen, "Seed Money," *Far Eastern Economic Review,* February 9, 1995.

91. Jack Epstein, "Reversing Its History, Bolivia Gives Power To Indigenous People," *Christian Science Monitor,* Feburary 16, 1995.

92. U.N. General Assembly, "Draft Programme of Action of the International Conference on Population and Development," New York, September 19, 1994; UNICEF and World Health Organization, New York and Geneva, private communications, February 17, 1994.

93. Amartya Sen, "The Economics of Life and Death," *Scientific American,* May 1993; Harald Muller, Director, Frankfurt Peace Research Institute, private communication, February 1991.

94. Wealthiest-country development assistance from Organization for Economic Co-operation and Development, "Sharp Changes in the Structure of Financial Flows to Developing Countries and Countries in Transition," press release, Paris, June 20, 1994; U.N. development and peacekeeping spending from Erskine Childers with Brian Urquhart, "Renewing the United Nations System," *Development Dialogue* (Dag Hammarskjöld Foundation/Ford Foundation), 1994:1; UNHCR budget from Heather Courtney, public information officer, UNHCR, Washington, D.C., private communication, October 4, 1994; UNDP budget from Ad de Rad, UNDP, New York, private communication, October 19, 1994.

95. Ian Steele, "Peacekeeping Gives UN Serious Money Troubles," *Depthnews Asia,* June 1994; UNDP, op. cit. note 55; Oscar-Jean N'Galamulume, "Arms Embargo, Food Aid Could Stay Zaire's Crisis," *Christian Science Monitor,* March 16, 1994.

PUBLICATION ORDER FORM

No. of
Copies

_____ 57. **Nuclear Power: The Market Test** by Christopher Flavin.
_____ 58. **Air Pollution, Acid Rain, and the Future of Forests** by Sandra Postel.
_____ 60. **Soil Erosion: Quiet Crisis in the World Economy** by Lester R. Brown and
          Edward C. Wolf.
_____ 61. **Electricity's Future: The Shift to Efficiency and Small-Scale Power**
          by Christopher Flavin.
_____ 63. **Energy Productivity: Key to Environmental Protection and Economic Progress**
          by William U. Chandler.
_____ 65. **Reversing Africa's Decline** by Lester R. Brown and Edward C. Wolf.
_____ 66. **World Oil: Coping With the Dangers of Success** by Christopher Flavin.
_____ 68. **Banishing Tobacco** by William U. Chandler.
_____ 70. **Electricity For A Developing World: New Directions** by Christopher Flavin.
_____ 71. **Altering the Earth's Chemistry: Assessing the Risks** by Sandra Postel.
_____ 75. **Reassessing Nuclear Power: The Fallout From Chernobyl** by Christopher Flavin.
_____ 77. **The Future of Urbanization: Facing the Ecological and Economic Constraints**
          by Lester R. Brown and Jodi L. Jacobson.
_____ 78. **On the Brink of Extinction: Conserving The Diversity of Life** by Edward C. Wolf.
_____ 79. **Defusing the Toxics Threat: Controlling Pesticides and Industrial Waste**
          by Sandra Postel.
_____ 80. **Planning the Global Family** by Jodi L. Jacobson.
_____ 81. **Renewable Energy: Today's Contribution, Tomorrow's Promise** by
          Cynthia Pollock Shea.
_____ 82. **Building on Success: The Age of Energy Efficiency** by Christopher Flavin
          and Alan B. Durning.
_____ 83. **Reforesting the Earth** by Sandra Postel and Lori Heise.
_____ 84. **Rethinking the Role of the Automobile** by Michael Renner.
_____ 86. **Environmental Refugees: A Yardstick of Habitability** by Jodi L. Jacobson.
_____ 88. **Action at the Grassroots: Fighting Poverty and Environmental Decline**
          by Alan B. Durning.
_____ 89. **National Security: The Economic and Environmental Dimensions** by Michael Renner.
_____ 90. **The Bicycle: Vehicle for a Small Planet** by Marcia D. Lowe.
_____ 91. **Slowing Global Warming: A Worldwide Strategy** by Christopher Flavin
_____ 92. **Poverty and the Environment: Reversing the Downward Spiral** by Alan B. Durning.
_____ 93. **Water for Agriculture: Facing the Limits** by Sandra Postel.
_____ 94. **Clearing the Air: A Global Agenda** by Hilary F. French.
_____ 95. **Apartheid's Environmental Toll** by Alan B. Durning.
_____ 96. **Swords Into Plowshares: Converting to a Peace Economy** by Michael Renner.
_____ 97. **The Global Politics of Abortion** by Jodi L. Jacobson.
_____ 98. **Alternatives to the Automobile: Transport for Livable Cities** by Marcia D. Lowe.
_____ 99. **Green Revolutions: Environmental Reconstruction in Eastern Europe and the
          Soviet Union** by Hilary F. French.
_____100. **Beyond the Petroleum Age: Designing a Solar Economy** by Christopher Flavin
          and Nicholas Lenssen.
_____101. **Discarding the Throwaway Society** by John E. Young.
_____102. **Women's Reproductive Health: The Silent Emergency** by Jodi L. Jacobson.
_____103. **Taking Stock: Animal Farming and the Environment** by Alan B. Durning and
          Holly B. Brough.
_____104. **Jobs in a Sustainable Economy** by Michael Renner.
_____105. **Shaping Cities: The Environmental and Human Dimensions** by Marcia D. Lowe.
_____106. **Nuclear Waste: The Problem That Won't Go Away** by Nicholas Lenssen.
_____107. **After the Earth Summit: The Future of Environmental Governance**
          by Hilary F. French.

_____ **Total Copies**

☐ **Single Copy: $5.00**

☐ **Bulk Copies (any combination of titles)**

　☐ 2–5: $4.00 ea.　　　☐ 6–20: $3.00 ea.　　　☐ 21 or more: $2.00 ea.

Call Director of Communication at (202) 452-1999 to inquire about discounts on larger orders.

☐ **Membership in the Worldwatch Library: $30.00 (international airmail $45.00)**

The paperback edition of our 250-page "annual physical of the planet,"
State of the World, plus all Worldwatch Papers released during the calendar year.

☐ **Worldwatch Database Disk: $89**

Includes up-to-the-minute global agricultural, energy, economic, environmental, social, and military indicators from all current Worldwatch publications.

Please check one: _____high-density IBM-compatible or _____Macintosh

---

☐ **Subscription to *World Watch* magazine: $20.00 (international airmail $35.00)**

Stay abreast of global environmental trends and issues with our award-winning, eminently readable bimonthly magazine.

Please include $3 postage and handling for non-subscription orders.

Make check payable to Worldwatch Institute

1776 Massachusetts Avenue, N.W., Washington, D.C. 20036-1904 USA

Enclosed is my check for U.S. $_____

VISA ☐　　Mastercard ☐ _____

　　　　　　　　　　Card Number　　　　　　　　　　　　　　Expiration Date

_____

name　　　　　　　　　　　　　　　　　　**daytime phone #**

_____

address

_____

city　　　　　　　　　　　　　**state**　　　**zip/country**　　　WWP

Phone: (202) 452-1999　　Fax: (202) 296-7365　　E-Mail: wwpub@igc.apc.org

PUBLICATION ORDER FORM

No. of
Copies

_____ 57. **Nuclear Power: The Market Test** by Christopher Flavin.

_____ 58. **Air Pollution, Acid Rain, and the Future of Forests** by Sandra Postel.

_____ 60. **Soil Erosion: Quiet Crisis in the World Economy** by Lester R. Brown and Edward C. Wolf.

_____ 61. **Electricity's Future: The Shift to Efficiency and Small-Scale Power** by Christopher Flavin.

_____ 63. **Energy Productivity: Key to Environmental Protection and Economic Progress** by William U. Chandler.

_____ 65. **Reversing Africa's Decline** by Lester R. Brown and Edward C. Wolf.

_____ 66. **World Oil: Coping With the Dangers of Success** by Christopher Flavin.

_____ 68. **Banishing Tobacco** by William U. Chandler.

_____ 70. **Electricity For A Developing World: New Directions** by Christopher Flavin.

_____ 71. **Altering the Earth's Chemistry: Assessing the Risks** by Sandra Postel.

_____ 75. **Reassessing Nuclear Power: The Fallout From Chernobyl** by Christopher Flavin.

_____ 77. **The Future of Urbanization: Facing the Ecological and Economic Constraints** by Lester R. Brown and Jodi L. Jacobson.

_____ 78. **On the Brink of Extinction: Conserving The Diversity of Life** by Edward C. Wolf.

_____ 79. **Defusing the Toxics Threat: Controlling Pesticides and Industrial Waste** by Sandra Postel.

_____ 80. **Planning the Global Family** by Jodi L. Jacobson.

_____ 81. **Renewable Energy: Today's Contribution, Tomorrow's Promise** by Cynthia Pollock Shea.

_____ 82. **Building on Success: The Age of Energy Efficiency** by Christopher Flavin and Alan B. Durning.

_____ 83. **Reforesting the Earth** by Sandra Postel and Lori Heise.

_____ 84. **Rethinking the Role of the Automobile** by Michael Renner.

_____ 86. **Environmental Refugees: A Yardstick of Habitability** by Jodi L. Jacobson.

_____ 88. **Action at the Grassroots: Fighting Poverty and Environmental Decline** by Alan B. Durning.

_____ 89. **National Security: The Economic and Environmental Dimensions** by Michael Renner.

_____ 90. **The Bicycle: Vehicle for a Small Planet** by Marcia D. Lowe.

_____ 91. **Slowing Global Warming: A Worldwide Strategy** by Christopher Flavin

_____ 92. **Poverty and the Environment: Reversing the Downward Spiral** by Alan B. Durning.

_____ 93. **Water for Agriculture: Facing the Limits** by Sandra Postel.

_____ 94. **Clearing the Air: A Global Agenda** by Hilary F. French.

_____ 95. **Apartheid's Environmental Toll** by Alan B. Durning.

_____ 96. **Swords Into Plowshares: Converting to a Peace Economy** by Michael Renner.

_____ 97. **The Global Politics of Abortion** by Jodi L. Jacobson.

_____ 98. **Alternatives to the Automobile: Transport for Livable Cities** by Marcia D. Lowe.

_____ 99. **Green Revolutions: Environmental Reconstruction in Eastern Europe and the Soviet Union** by Hilary F. French.

_____ 100. **Beyond the Petroleum Age: Designing a Solar Economy** by Christopher Flavin and Nicholas Lenssen.

_____ 101. **Discarding the Throwaway Society** by John E. Young.

_____ 102. **Women's Reproductive Health: The Silent Emergency** by Jodi L. Jacobson.

_____ 103. **Taking Stock: Animal Farming and the Environment** by Alan B. Durning and Holly B. Brough.

_____ 104. **Jobs in a Sustainable Economy** by Michael Renner.

_____ 105. **Shaping Cities: The Environmental and Human Dimensions** by Marcia D. Lowe.

_____ 106. **Nuclear Waste: The Problem That Won't Go Away** by Nicholas Lenssen.

_____ 107. **After the Earth Summit: The Future of Environmental Governance** by Hilary F. French.

_____ **Total Copies**

☐ **Single Copy: $5.00**

☐ **Bulk Copies (any combination of titles)**
   ☐ 2–5: $4.00 ea.   ☐ 6–20: $3.00 ea.   ☐ 21 or more: $2.00 ea.
   Call Director of Communication at (202) 452-1999 to inquire about discounts on larger
   orders.

☐ **Membership in the Worldwatch Library: $30.00 (international airmail $45.00)**
   The paperback edition of our 250-page "annual physical of the planet,"
   State of the World, plus all Worldwatch Papers released during the calendar year.

☐ **Worldwatch Database Disk: $89**
Includes up-to-the-minute global agricultural, energy, economic, environmental, social,
and military indicators from all current Worldwatch publications.

Please check one: _____high-density IBM-compatible or   _____Macintosh

---

☐ **Subscription to *World Watch* magazine: $20.00 (international airmail $35.00)**
   Stay abreast of global environmental trends and issues with our award-winning,
   eminently readable bimonthly magazine.

Please include $3 postage and handling for non-subscription orders.

Make check payable to Worldwatch Institute
1776 Massachusetts Avenue, N.W., Washington, D.C. 20036-1904 USA

Enclosed is my check for U.S. $_____

VISA ☐   Mastercard ☐   _____
                                   Card Number   Expiration Date

_____
name   **daytime phone #**

_____
address

_____
city   **state**   **zip/country**   WWP

Phone: (202) 452-1999   Fax: (202) 296-7365   E-Mail: wwpub@igc.apc.org

PUBLICATION ORDER FORM

No. of
Copies

_____ 57. **Nuclear Power: The Market Test** by Christopher Flavin.

_____ 58. **Air Pollution, Acid Rain, and the Future of Forests** by Sandra Postel.

_____ 60. **Soil Erosion: Quiet Crisis in the World Economy** by Lester R. Brown and
Edward C. Wolf.

_____ 61. **Electricity's Future: The Shift to Efficiency and Small-Scale Power**
by Christopher Flavin.

_____ 63. **Energy Productivity: Key to Environmental Protection and Economic Progress**
by William U. Chandler.

_____ 65. **Reversing Africa's Decline** by Lester R. Brown and Edward C. Wolf.

_____ 66. **World Oil: Coping With the Dangers of Success** by Christopher Flavin.

_____ 68. **Banishing Tobacco** by William U. Chandler.

_____ 70. **Electricity For A Developing World: New Directions** by Christopher Flavin.

_____ 71. **Altering the Earth's Chemistry: Assessing the Risks** by Sandra Postel.

_____ 75. **Reassessing Nuclear Power: The Fallout From Chernobyl** by Christopher Flavin.

_____ 77. **The Future of Urbanization: Facing the Ecological and Economic Constraints**
by Lester R. Brown and Jodi L. Jacobson.

_____ 78. **On the Brink of Extinction: Conserving The Diversity of Life** by Edward C. Wolf.

_____ 79. **Defusing the Toxics Threat: Controlling Pesticides and Industrial Waste**
by Sandra Postel.

_____ 80. **Planning the Global Family** by Jodi L. Jacobson.

_____ 81. **Renewable Energy: Today's Contribution, Tomorrow's Promise** by
Cynthia Pollock Shea.

_____ 82. **Building on Success: The Age of Energy Efficiency** by Christopher Flavin
and Alan B. Durning.

_____ 83. **Reforesting the Earth** by Sandra Postel and Lori Heise.

_____ 84. **Rethinking the Role of the Automobile** by Michael Renner.

_____ 86. **Environmental Refugees: A Yardstick of Habitability** by Jodi L. Jacobson.

_____ 88. **Action at the Grassroots: Fighting Poverty and Environmental Decline**
by Alan B. Durning.

_____ 89. **National Security: The Economic and Environmental Dimensions** by Michael Renner.

_____ 90. **The Bicycle: Vehicle for a Small Planet** by Marcia D. Lowe.

_____ 91. **Slowing Global Warming: A Worldwide Strategy** by Christopher Flavin

_____ 92. **Poverty and the Environment: Reversing the Downward Spiral** by Alan B. Durning.

_____ 93. **Water for Agriculture: Facing the Limits** by Sandra Postel.

_____ 94. **Clearing the Air: A Global Agenda** by Hilary F. French.

_____ 95. **Apartheid's Environmental Toll** by Alan B. Durning.

_____ 96. **Swords Into Plowshares: Converting to a Peace Economy** by Michael Renner.

_____ 97. **The Global Politics of Abortion** by Jodi L. Jacobson.

_____ 98. **Alternatives to the Automobile: Transport for Livable Cities** by Marcia D. Lowe.

_____ 99. **Green Revolutions: Environmental Reconstruction in Eastern Europe and the
Soviet Union** by Hilary F. French.

_____100. **Beyond the Petroleum Age: Designing a Solar Economy** by Christopher Flavin
and Nicholas Lenssen.

_____101. **Discarding the Throwaway Society** by John E. Young.

_____102. **Women's Reproductive Health: The Silent Emergency** by Jodi L. Jacobson.

_____103. **Taking Stock: Animal Farming and the Environment** by Alan B. Durning and
Holly B. Brough.

_____104. **Jobs in a Sustainable Economy** by Michael Renner.

_____105. **Shaping Cities: The Environmental and Human Dimensions** by Marcia D. Lowe.

_____106. **Nuclear Waste: The Problem That Won't Go Away** by Nicholas Lenssen.

_____107. **After the Earth Summit: The Future of Environmental Governance**
by Hilary F. French.

_____ **Total Copies**

☐ **Single Copy: $5.00**

☐ **Bulk Copies (any combination of titles)**

    ☐ 2–5: $4.00 ea.   ☐ 6–20: $3.00 ea.   ☐ 21 or more: $2.00 ea.

    Call Director of Communication at (202) 452-1999 to inquire about discounts on larger orders.

☐ **Membership in the Worldwatch Library: $30.00 (international airmail $45.00)**

    The paperback edition of our 250-page "annual physical of the planet," *State of the World,* plus all Worldwatch Papers released during the calendar year.

☐ **Worldwatch Database Disk: $89**

Includes up-to-the-minute global agricultural, energy, economic, environmental, social, and military indicators from all current Worldwatch publications.

Please check one: _____high-density IBM-compatible or _____Macintosh

---

☐ **Subscription to *World Watch* magazine: $20.00 (international airmail $35.00)**

    Stay abreast of global environmental trends and issues with our award-winning, eminently readable bimonthly magazine.

Please include $3 postage and handling for non-subscription orders.

Make check payable to Worldwatch Institute
1776 Massachusetts Avenue, N.W., Washington, D.C. 20036-1904 USA

Enclosed is my check for U.S. $_____

VISA ☐   Mastercard ☐ _____

                          Card Number   Expiration Date

---

name   **daytime phone #**

---

address

---

city   **state**   **zip/country**   WWP

Phone: (202) 452-1999   Fax: (202) 296-7365   E-Mail: wwpub@igc.apc.org

PUBLICATION ORDER FORM

No. of
Copies

_____ 57. **Nuclear Power: The Market Test** by Christopher Flavin.
_____ 58. **Air Pollution, Acid Rain, and the Future of Forests** by Sandra Postel.
_____ 60. **Soil Erosion: Quiet Crisis in the World Economy** by Lester R. Brown and
        Edward C. Wolf.
_____ 61. **Electricity's Future: The Shift to Efficiency and Small-Scale Power**
        by Christopher Flavin.
_____ 63. **Energy Productivity: Key to Environmental Protection and Economic Progress**
        by William U. Chandler.
_____ 65. **Reversing Africa's Decline** by Lester R. Brown and Edward C. Wolf.
_____ 66. **World Oil: Coping With the Dangers of Success** by Christopher Flavin.
_____ 68. **Banishing Tobacco** by William U. Chandler.
_____ 70. **Electricity For A Developing World: New Directions** by Christopher Flavin.
_____ 71. **Altering the Earth's Chemistry: Assessing the Risks** by Sandra Postel.
_____ 75. **Reassessing Nuclear Power: The Fallout From Chernobyl** by Christopher Flavin.
_____ 77. **The Future of Urbanization: Facing the Ecological and Economic Constraints**
        by Lester R. Brown and Jodi L. Jacobson.
_____ 78. **On the Brink of Extinction: Conserving The Diversity of Life** by Edward C. Wolf.
_____ 79. **Defusing the Toxics Threat: Controlling Pesticides and Industrial Waste**
        by Sandra Postel.
_____ 80. **Planning the Global Family** by Jodi L. Jacobson.
_____ 81. **Renewable Energy: Today's Contribution, Tomorrow's Promise** by
        Cynthia Pollock Shea.
_____ 82. **Building on Success: The Age of Energy Efficiency** by Christopher Flavin
        and Alan B. Durning.
_____ 83. **Reforesting the Earth** by Sandra Postel and Lori Heise.
_____ 84. **Rethinking the Role of the Automobile** by Michael Renner.
_____ 86. **Environmental Refugees: A Yardstick of Habitability** by Jodi L. Jacobson.
_____ 88. **Action at the Grassroots: Fighting Poverty and Environmental Decline**
        by Alan B. Durning.
_____ 89. **National Security: The Economic and Environmental Dimensions** by Michael Renner.
_____ 90. **The Bicycle: Vehicle for a Small Planet** by Marcia D. Lowe.
_____ 91. **Slowing Global Warming: A Worldwide Strategy** by Christopher Flavin
_____ 92. **Poverty and the Environment: Reversing the Downward Spiral** by Alan B. Durning.
_____ 93. **Water for Agriculture: Facing the Limits** by Sandra Postel.
_____ 94. **Clearing the Air: A Global Agenda** by Hilary F. French.
_____ 95. **Apartheid's Environmental Toll** by Alan B. Durning.
_____ 96. **Swords Into Plowshares: Converting to a Peace Economy** by Michael Renner.
_____ 97. **The Global Politics of Abortion** by Jodi L. Jacobson.
_____ 98. **Alternatives to the Automobile: Transport for Livable Cities** by Marcia D. Lowe.
_____ 99. **Green Revolutions: Environmental Reconstruction in Eastern Europe and the
        Soviet Union** by Hilary F. French.
_____ 100. **Beyond the Petroleum Age: Designing a Solar Economy** by Christopher Flavin
        and Nicholas Lenssen.
_____ 101. **Discarding the Throwaway Society** by John E. Young.
_____ 102. **Women's Reproductive Health: The Silent Emergency** by Jodi L. Jacobson.
_____ 103. **Taking Stock: Animal Farming and the Environment** by Alan B. Durning and
        Holly B. Brough.
_____ 104. **Jobs in a Sustainable Economy** by Michael Renner.
_____ 105. **Shaping Cities: The Environmental and Human Dimensions** by Marcia D. Lowe.
_____ 106. **Nuclear Waste: The Problem That Won't Go Away** by Nicholas Lenssen.
_____ 107. **After the Earth Summit: The Future of Environmental Governance**
        by Hilary F. French.

_____ **Total Copies**

☐ **Single Copy: $5.00**
☐ **Bulk Copies (any combination of titles)**
   ☐ 2–5: $4.00 ea.   ☐ 6–20: $3.00 ea.   ☐ 21 or more: $2.00 ea.
   Call Director of Communication at (202) 452-1999 to inquire about discounts on larger orders.
☐ **Membership in the Worldwatch Library: $30.00 (international airmail $45.00)**
   The paperback edition of our 250-page "annual physical of the planet,"
   State of the World, plus all Worldwatch Papers released during the calendar year.

☐ **Worldwatch Database Disk: $89**
Includes up-to-the-minute global agricultural, energy, economic, environmental, social, and military indicators from all current Worldwatch publications.

Please check one: _____high-density IBM-compatible or   _____Macintosh

---

☐ **Subscription to *World Watch* magazine: $20.00 (international airmail $35.00)**
   Stay abreast of global environmental trends and issues with our award-winning, eminently readable bimonthly magazine.

Please include $3 postage and handling for non-subscription orders.

Make check payable to Worldwatch Institute
1776 Massachusetts Avenue, N.W., Washington, D.C. 20036-1904 USA

Enclosed is my check for U.S. $_____
VISA ☐   Mastercard ☐ _____
                           Card Number   Expiration Date

_____
name   **daytime phone #**

_____
address

_____
city   **state**   **zip/country**   WWP
Phone: (202) 452-1999   Fax: (202) 296-7365   E-Mail: wwpub@igc.apc.org